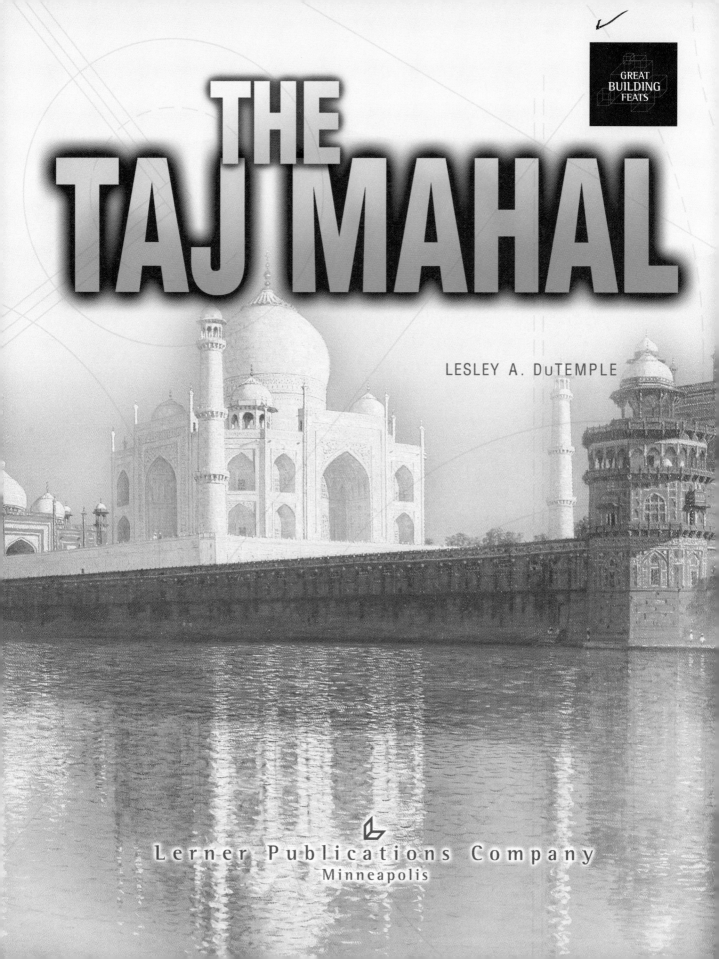

THE TAJ MAHAL

LESLEY A. DuTEMPLE

GREAT
BUILDING
FEATS

Lerner Publications Company
Minneapolis

For my father, with love

Lerner Publications Company
A division of Lerner Publishing Group
241 First Avenue North
Minneapolis, Minnesota 55401

Website address: www.lernerbooks.com

Library of Congress Cataloging-in-Publication Data

DuTemple, Lesley A.
    The Taj Mahal / by Lesley A. DuTemple.
        p.   cm. — (Great building feats)
    Summary: Recounts the history of the creation of the Taj Mahal, built as a tomb and memorial for the wife of the Mughal emperor Shah Jahan.
    Includes bibliographical references and index.
    ISBN: 0–8225–4694–9 (lib. bdg. : alk. paper)
    1. Taj Mahal (Agra, India)—Juvenile literature. 2. Architecture, Mughal—India—Agra—Juvenile literature. 3. Agra (India)—Buildings, structures, etc.—Juvenile literature. [1. Taj Mahal (Agra, India)] I. Title. II. Series.
    NA6008.A33 D88 2003
    726'.8'09542—dc21   2002151380

Manufactured in the United States of America
1 2 3 4 5 6 – JR – 08 07 06 05 04 03

CONTENTS

ABOUT GREAT BUILDING FEATS

HUMANS HAVE LONG SOUGHT to make their mark on the world. From the ancient Great Wall of China to the ultramodern Channel Tunnel linking Great Britain and France, grand structures reveal how people have tried to express themselves and better their lives.

Great structures have served a number of purposes. Sometimes they met a practical need. For example, the New York subway system makes getting around a huge city easier. Other structures reflected spiritual beliefs. The Pantheon in Rome, Italy, was created as a temple to Roman gods and later became a Catholic church. Sometimes we

Shah Jahan *(above)*, the fifth emperor of the Mughal Empire, commissioned the building of the Taj Mahal *(right)* as a tomb for his beloved wife.

can only guess at the story behind a structure. The purpose of Stonehenge in England eludes us, and perhaps it always will.

This book is one in a series of books called Great Building Feats. Each book in the series takes a close look at some of the most amazing building feats around the world. Each of them posed a unique set of engineering and geographical problems. In many cases, these problems seemed nearly insurmountable when construction began.

More than a compilation of facts, the Great Building Feats series not only describes how each structure was built but also why. Each project called forth the best minds of its time. Many people invested their all in the outcome. Their lives are as much a part of the structure as the earth and stone used in its construction. Finally, each structure in the Great

Building Feats series remains a dynamic feature of the modern world, still amazing users and viewers as well as historians.

A MONUMENT TO LOVE

India's Taj Mahal is a beautiful example of a great building feat. With the exception of its gardens, the Taj Mahal of modern times is exactly as it was designed in 1631. It was built by Shah Jahan, the fifth emperor of the Mughal (sometimes called the Mogul) Empire. The Mughal Empire lasted from about 1526 until 1858 and included most of present-day India, Pakistan, and Afghanistan. The Taj Mahal is a complex of buildings—a mosque, a guest house, an enormous entrance gate, four minaret towers, and the tomb of Mumtaz Mahal, Shah Jahan's favorite wife. It is laid out in a rectangular grid on 42 acres (17 hectares) along the Yamuna River, with water fountains, gardens, and reflecting pools,

The Taj Mahal was built in the city of Agra, India, at the height of the Mughal Empire. Shah Jahan, whose name means "King of the World," was one of the richest men on earth. "There were literally trunks of jewels in the imperial treasury," according to historian Milo Beach, "trunks of emeralds, sapphires, rubies, and diamonds." Shah Jahan had palaces scattered like gemstones across his far-flung empire.

About twenty thousand people worked on the Taj Mahal. Many skilled craftsmen, such as

The Taj Mahal is in Agra, a city in India, which was part of the Mughal Empire in the seventeenth century.

EUROPE

ASIA

AFRICA

Agra

INDIA

ARABIAN SEA

Equator

INDIAN OCEAN

stonecutters, bricklayers, and calligraphers, moved to Agra to work on the project. Elephants and oxen hauled tons of marble more than 200 miles (322 kilometers) to the site. Brickmakers produced thousands of bricks. Wagonloads of colorful gemstones arrived from all parts of Asia and Europe.

The story of the Taj Mahal is one of great passion and sorrow. Shah Jahan built it as a tomb for his beloved Mumtaz Mahal, whose beauty inspired many royal poets. He chose to express his grief through architecture. The Taj Mahal is a testament to his undying love.

Few documents have survived from this period of history, so many facts regarding the Taj Mahal remain shrouded in mystery. The few records that are available offer conflicting facts, making it difficult for historians to determine the truth. For example, some documents say that the Taj Mahal took eleven years to build. Others say the project took as long as twenty-two years.

Another problem is that the point of view in the surviving documents is suspect. Shah Jahan employed several court historians to document his reign, and their accounts aren't entirely reliable. They recorded things that showed the emperor in a good light, as a perfect husband, father, and ruler. Accounts by Europeans who visited India during Shah Jahan's reign paint a less flattering picture of him.

The mystery surrounding the Taj Mahal does not dim its beauty, however. It has been called one of the wonders of the world. In modern times, millions of visitors journey to India every year to see the tomb, its grounds, and the buildings around it. Sixty thousand people visit the site every day, making it one of the most popular tourist attractions in the world. They find an extraordinary white marble building, shimmering like a jewel on the banks of the Yamuna River—the famous Taj Mahal, tangible evidence of a love story that has endured for centuries.

Chapter One

THE CHOSEN ONE OF THE PALACE

(1519–1631)

A HOT, DRY WIND BLEW through the military encampment outside the city of Burhanpur in south-central India in a region known as the Deccan. Swirls of sand skittered around the tents, and a shimmering heat mirage floated on the horizon, blending into the bleached blue sky. It was June 16, 1631, and Shah Jahan, the fifth emperor of the Mughal Empire, was about to crush a rebellion led by the traitor Khan Jahan Lodi. Thousands of imperial soldiers were camped on the dusty plain. The war against Khan Jahan Lodi

Above, This is one artist's conception of Mumtaz Mahal, Shah Jehan's favorite wife. She accompanied Shah Jahan when he went into battles, such as the one depicted in this Mughal miniature painting *(right).*

had been going on for months, and everyone was anxious to get back to Agra, one of several cities in which Shah Jahan maintained a residence. Thankfully, victory seemed near.

One tent in the midst of the military encampment stood out. Draped in elaborate folds of silk, it was the tent of Mumtaz Mahal, Shah Jahan's wife of nineteen years and empress of the Mughal Empire. Court historians recorded her beauty, her lustrous hair, and dark eyes. "The moon hid its face in shame before her," one historian wrote. Inside her sumptuous tent, surrounded by rich tapestries and other comforts, the empress was about to give birth to her fourteenth child.

Shah Jahan spent the day directing troops and conducting state business, while anxiously awaiting news of his wife. Finally, one of her messengers arrived to announce the birth of a healthy baby girl. There was no word of Mumtaz Mahal herself, however. Irritated, Shah Jahan sent one of his own messengers to her tent. Hours passed, but the messenger didn't return.

It was past midnight, and Shah Jahan was preparing to go to

Mumtaz Mahal when a messenger from the empress arrived. The messenger said she was very tired and wished to rest undisturbed for the remainder of the night. Relieved, Shah Jahan went to bed.

A few hours later, Shah Jahan was awakened by another messenger. The empress was calling for him. He dressed immediately and hurried to her tent. Inside her elegant quarters, Mumtaz Mahal was dying. Her devoted doctor, Wazir Khan, took Shah Jahan aside and said that before Mumtaz Mahal had given birth, she had heard her unborn child cry out in her womb. In seventeenth-century India, this was a sign, a bad omen. It meant there was no hope for Mumtaz Mahal.

Shah Jahan immediately dismissed everyone except Wazir Khan and his wife's head lady-in-waiting, Satti al-Nisa Khanam. Then he sat next to Mumtaz Mahal, holding her in his arms for the remaining hours of the night. On June 17, 1631, she died just before the sun rose.

Mumtaz Mahal died in her grieving husband's arms.

As one poet described the scene, Shah Jahan "cried out with grief, like an ocean raging with storm." He secluded himself in his tent. For eight days he refused all food and visitors. His attendants, posted outside his door, heard only a low, continuous moan.

On the ninth day, Shah Jahan emerged from his tent. Kalim, one of Shah Jahan's court historians, wrote: "His tearful eyes sought help from spectacles, for his eyesight had decreased from weeping." According to Kalim, Shah Jahan's grief had noticeably aged him. "In his beard before this, no white hairs did the eyes see, except a few," wrote Kalim. "But in this paining of the heart, most turned . . . white."

> Shah Jahan "cried out with grief, like an ocean raging with storm."
>
> —**court poet**

LOVE AT FIRST SIGHT

Mumtaz Mahal and Shah Jahan had met about twenty-four years earlier, in 1607. She was fifteen, and her name then had been Arjumand Banu Baygam. He was sixteen, and he was called Prince Khurram.

They met at one of the royal bazaars staged by the women of the royal court. Men of the court came and bought things from the booths. Mumtaz Mahal, the daughter of a high-ranking family, was running one of the booths at the bazaar.

As the teenaged son of the reigning emperor, Shah Jahan was considered quite a catch. He was confident and handsome, with jet-black hair and a neatly trimmed beard. As he strode through the bazaar, stopping to look at various booths, girls giggled and flirted with him. He stopped at Mumtaz Mahal's booth and bought a large piece of glass shaped like a diamond. Although the meeting between the two teenagers lasted only a few minutes, it was love at first sight for both of them.

The next day Shah Jahan asked his father, the Emperor Jahangir, for permission to marry. As a Muslim, Shah Jahan would be allowed to have four wives. But Mughal emperors didn't marry for love. They married to cement political relationships and to acquire more wealth. The Emperor

Musicians in this painting are playing at a royal wedding, such as that of Mumtaz Mahal and Shah Jahan.

Jahangir gave his consent but insisted that the young couple wait five years. He also insisted that Shah Jahan first marry a princess from the neighboring country of Persia to cement political ties.

For the next five years, Shah Jahan and Mumtaz Mahal were not permitted to see each other. Yet they never stopped loving each other, and they eagerly waited for the day when they could marry.

When they finally married on March 27, 1612, she instantly became his favorite wife and constant companion. The title he gave her, Mumtaz Mahal, means "chosen one of the palace," proclaiming her special place in his heart.

Mumtaz Mahal accompanied Shah Jahan everywhere, even traveling with him on military campaigns. Her compassion toward the poor had endeared her to the Indian people. She was known for compiling lists of widows and orphans and making sure that Shah Jahan took care of them. As the granddaughter of Jahangir's prime minister, the daughter of Shah Jahan's prime minister-to-be, and the niece of the former empress, Muntaz Mahal had never experienced poverty. Yet she distributed coins and food to the poor almost every day. Shah Jahan entrusted Mumtaz Mahal with the keeping of the state seal. Once a document was stamped with it, not even the emperor could reverse its authority.

Over the years, the couple had fourteen children. Seven survived beyond childbirth. Mumtaz Mahal was pregnant when Shah Jahan was ready to leave for Burhanpur in the spring of 1631, but he took her with him. Like all Mughal emperors, Shah Jahan was Muslim. After Mumtaz Mahal's death, he buried her immediately, according to Muslim religious custom. He visited her grave every Friday night, the evening of the Islamic holy day.

Then in December 1631, the war against Khan Jahan Lodi was won. The tents were disassembled, and preparations were made to return to Agra. Shah Jahan refused to leave Mumtaz Mahal behind. In violation of Muslim burial law, he had her body disinterred. The return to Agra would be both a triumphant military procession and a grieving funeral procession.

Shah Jahan was already planning a permanent tomb for his wife in Agra. He was determined to build a tomb that was not only fitting for the love of his life but also fitting for the empress of a mighty and glorious empire.

THE BEGINNING OF THE MUGHAL EMPIRE

The Mughals were descendants of Timur, also referred to as Tamerlane—a leader of a Turkish-speaking tribe that was allied with the Mongols and lived in the area around present-day Uzbekistan. Timur conquered a large part of Central Asia. His descendants gradually moved southward toward present-day Afghanistan.

One of Timur's descendents, Babur, was born in 1483 in Fergana, in the high arid lands north of present-day Afghanistan. Babur's father, the king of Fergana, died in 1494, and Babur became king, even though he was only eleven years old.

In 1519 Babur looked for a larger empire to rule. He gathered a small army and moved through a pass in the Hindu Kush mountain range, north of present-day Pakistan. Finally, in 1526, with only twelve thousand men, he defeated an army of one hundred thousand men, the forces of a local

Timur, or Tamerlane, the feared leader of the Mongols, was an ancestor of Babur.

prince. He took control of two important river valleys, the Indus and Ganges, in present-day northern Pakistan and India. With the conquest of these vast river valleys, Babur established the Mughal Empire and began more than 330 years of Mughal rule in the region. This area's religion was primarily Hindu, while its Mughal conquerors were Muslims. During the reigns of Babur and his son, the two religious groups often clashed.

The second Mughal emperor, Babur's son, Humayun, became emperor in 1530 after Babur's death. He quickly managed to lose nearly all the territory his father had acquired. He spent much of his reign wandering in the desert, mustering troops, and fighting to regain his father's lands and to reestablish himself on the throne.

BABUR AND HUMAYUN

While in Agra, Babur's son, Humayun, became deathly ill. No matter what court doctors tried, Humayun didn't respond, and they abandoned all hope of recovery. Then a wise man told Babur that a person could obtain anything, provided he gave up his most prized possession for it. Babur decided that his most prized possession was his own life. Promising his life to God, Babur circled Humayun's bed three times, repeating his promise each time. Within days Humayun had recovered. Within months Babur died. No one knew the cause.

Babur had conquered India, but he called it "a country of few charms." He had no desire to be buried there. His body was taken back to Kabul, Afghanistan, and placed in a crypt in his favorite garden—one he had designed. The crypt can still be seen about fifty feet (15 meters) from a mosque (Muslim building for prayer) his great-great-grandson, Shah Jahan, built to honor him one hundred years after he died.

Babur *(seated, center)* became king of Fergana when he was eleven. But he looked for larger lands to rule and took control of most of what is now Afghanistan, Pakistan, and India.

The Mughal Empire 1556–1707

PERSIA (IRAN)

Shiraz

(UZBEKISTAN)

Fergana

(AFGHANISTAN)

HINDU KUSH

Kabul

CHINA

Lahore

(PAKISTAN)

Indus River

HIMALAYAS

Shahjahnabad (Delhi)

Yamuna River

Fatehpur-Sikri

Makrana

Jaipur

Akbarabad (Agra)

Ganges River

INDIA

Kolkatta

Burhanpur

ARABIAN SEA

N

DECCAN

BAY OF BENGAL

Miles
0   200   400

0   200 400 600
Kilometers

At its height, the Mughal Empire stretched from present-day Afghanistan to the southern end of the Indian subcontinent.

Humayun finally succeeded. But in 1556, one year after regaining his empire, he was relaxing on the terrace of his library in his capital city of Delhi when the Muslim call to evening prayer was sounded. He rose, tripped on the hem of his cloak, and toppled down a flight of stone stairs. Within hours he was dead. His thirteen-year-old son, Akbar, became the third Mughal emperor.

Akbar inherited an empire full of warring tribes and different religious groups—none of whom liked being conquered by the Mughals. But Akbar was convinced that this large territory could be united into something truly great.

HOW THE EMPERORS GOT THEIR NAMES

Only men could rule the Mughal Empire. When a Mughal prince became emperor, he often took a new name. This tradition began with Babur. His throne name was Zahirud-Din Muhammad. As the conqueror of India, he adopted the name Babur, which means "the Tiger."

Shah Jahan's father was originally named Salim. When he became emperor, Prince Salim assumed the name Jahangir, which means the "King Who Seizes the World." As Jahangir's son, Shah Jahan was known as Prince Khurram. Shah Jahan means "King of the World." His father gave him this title before he became emperor (a tribute that had never before been paid to an uncrowned emperor) in honor of his military victories.

The Mughal Empire encompassed many different tribes, nations, and religions. Throne names reflected this melting pot, since from emperor to emperor, the languages used for throne names changed. Babur's throne name was Arabic, while Jahangir's and Shah Jahan's were Persian.

Akbar fought wars and conquered almost all of India, but in his empire different religious groups were allowed to practice their religions in peace. He even married at least one Hindu princess. Akbar also wanted to learn about other religions. He invited two Catholic priests to his palace so he could quiz them and learn about Catholicism. Because of his religious tolerance, he ruled more easily than his ancestors had.

Akbar put down an unsuccessful rebellion staged against him by his son Jahangir and died peacefully in 1605. Jahangir, his rebellious son, became the fourth Mughal emperor. Jahangir's reign started off well. He guaranteed people the right to government hospitals and freedom from unfair tax rules. He abolished harsh punishments, such as slicing off the nose for a petty crime. Gradually, though, it became apparent that Jahangir was a very erratic ruler, an alcoholic, and an opium addict. He killed another man, then married his wife. It is said that this wife, Nur Jahan, really controlled the kingdom.

Jahangir died in 1627 at the age of fifty-eight, and his son, Shah Jahan, succeeded him as the fifth Mughal emperor in 1628—after the suspicious deaths of all four of his brothers. The Mughal line of succession was often bloody. Shah Jahan's older brother had rebelled against Jahangir, and even Shah Jahan would ultimately be overthrown and

The gold and gem-studded Peacock Throne was a symbol of Shah Jahan's wealth and power.

imprisoned by one of his and Mumtaz Mahal's sons. Mughal princes killed each other off because there was much wealth and power at stake.

MUGHAL WEALTH

The Mughals were fantastically wealthy. With each region they conquered, they acquired more treasure. With each new village under their control, more tax monies were added to the royal treasury. Shah Jahan was emperor of what may have been the wealthiest empire in the world at that time.

One of Shah Jahan's treasure houses contained "750 pounds of pearls, 275 pounds of emeralds, 5,000 gems from Cathay, corals, topazes, and other less precious stones in almost infinite number, 200 daggers, 1,000 gold studded saddles with jewels, 2 golden thrones, 3 silver thrones, 100 silver chairs, 5 golden chairs, 200 most precious mirrors, 100,000 precious silver plates and utensils, 50,000 pounds of gold plate, wrought gold and silver, Chinese vessels, worked necklaces, cups, discs, candelabra, tubs of uncut diamonds, gold images of elephants, golden bridles, porcelain vessels."

FATEHPUR SIKRI

Only sons were allowed to succeed Mughal emperors to the throne. Thirteen years into his reign, Akbar still had none. Seeking help, Akbar consulted a wise man living in Sikri, 23 miles (37 km) west of Agra. Shaikh Salim Chisti recited blessings and promised that the emperor would have a son. Shortly after, one of Akbar's wives gave birth to Prince Salim (later called Jahangir).

Akbar was so grateful to Shaikh Salim Chisti that he ordered an entire city built at the site of the wise man's retreat. Akbar's plan for the new city of Fatehpur Sikri included three palaces (separate ones for his Hindu and Muslim wives), a five-story mosque, waterworks, numerous private residences, a mint for stamping coins, the first Indian hospital, a zoo, and an artificial lake. A wall with nine gates surrounded much of the city.

Builders work on construction of the city of Fatehpur Sikri.

It took seven years to build Fatehpur Sikri. Akbar used the city as an official residence for fifteen years. Then he suddenly abandoned it in 1585. No one knows why, but the city may have suffered a shortage of water. The ruins of Fatehpur Sikri can still be seen west of Agra.

This describes only a portion of his wealth. The treasure house in Lahore, India, was said to contain three times as much. Mughal emperors covered themselves in jewels and passed out trays of rubies and diamonds during court festivities.

THE RED FORT IN AGRA

Instead of a single capital city, Mughal emperors used at least four Indian cities as primary residences: Agra, Delhi, Fatehpur Sikri, and Lahore. All four cities contained elaborate palace complexes (a grouping of structures) called forts.

The palace complex located near the Yamuna River in Agra is called the Red Fort. Built by Akbar between 1565 and 1574, it is a huge complex of buildings. It is surrounded by two massive red sandstone walls, which stretch 1.5 miles (2.4 km) in a semicircle. Gold and silver covered the palace ceilings. Precious stones decorated its walls.

Thousands of people lived at the Red Fort during the reign of Jahangir. Five thousand women lived in the harem, an area or building just for women. Twelve thousand elephants, one hundred tame lions, three thousand camels, and thousands of other animals were also maintained there.

Shah Jahan lived at the Red Fort when his grandfather Akbar was emperor and also when his father Jahangir was emperor. The bazaar where he met Mumtaz Mahal was held inside the Red Fort. When Shah Jahan left the battlefield at Burhanpur, it was to Agra and the Red Fort that he returned. And it was in Agra, within sight of the Red Fort, that Mumtaz Mahal would be buried.

Shah Jahan grew up at the palace complex known as the Red Fort in Agra. It was built by his grandfather, Akbar.

Chapter Two
THE ORIGINS OF THE TAJ MAHAL
(1562–1632)

ON DECEMBER 15, 1631, THE body of Mumtaz Mahal left Burhanpur and began the long journey to Agra, 435 miles (700 km) away. The somber funeral procession was led by fifteen-year-old Prince Shah Shuja, Shah Jahan and Mumtaz Mahal's third child and second oldest son.

Everyone in the procession was dressed in white, the Muslim color of mourning. The royal family and nobility rode on enormous elephants, covered in cloths of gold

This royal procession is very much like the funeral procession that brought Mumtaz Mahal's body back to Agra.

and velvet. Thousands of soldiers carried white banners and marched in solemn formation. In the center of the procession, the body of the empress rode on a gold, canopied litter (a kind of couch) carried by ten soldiers.

In honor of Mumtaz Mahal's compassion for the poor, Shah Jahan ordered "that all along the way, every day abundant food and innumerable silver and gold coins should be given to the needy and indigent."

Every section of the route was lined with mourners. Farmers, merchants, housewives, and children clustered at the edge of the road. As the empress's body passed by, the crowds broke into weeping and wailing.

LAND FOR THE TOMB

Mumtaz Mahal's tomb was going to be built on the banks of the Yamuna River, within sight of the Red Fort in Agra. A nobleman, Raja Jai Singh, owned one of the most beautiful pieces of land in Agra, set on a bend of the river. It was a large tract inherited from his grandfather, who had been a great friend of the emperor Akbar. Raja Jai Singh donated it to Shah Jahan for the site of Mumtaz Muhal's tomb.

It would have been an honor just to donate land for the empress's tomb, but two court historians record that Shah Jahan gave Raja Jai Singh a "lofty mansion" in return. Another historical document records that Raja Jai Singh received four houses in return for the land along the Yamuna River.

The procession reached Agra on January 8, 1632. Mumtaz Mahal's body was temporarily buried on the land received from Raja Jai Singh. Nearby, construction on her tomb had already begun.

THE ARCHITECT OF THE TAJ MAHAL

All Mughal emperors built lavishly, but Shah Jahan was especially noted for his architectural achievements. He was interested in all the arts, but architecture was his primary love. With the death of his favorite wife, he focused even more on architecture. In the six months since her death, he and several of his architects had worked out the plans for the Taj Mahal.

A designer holding a grid plan oversees garden construction. Shah Jahan worked with several designers and architects to design the Taj Mahal complex. No one knows for sure who they were.

No single person designed the whole Taj Mahal complex. The buildings were the work of many people—architects, engineers, artists, calligraphers, and Shah Jahan himself. Only one document names an architect for the Taj Mahal, but it was written by the son of the architect named Ustad Ahmad Lahori (not the same Lahori who was Shah Jahan's historian). No other evidence backs up this claim. Ustad Ahmad Lahori was a well known architect of the time, and Shah Jahan employed him for other projects (including the Shahjahanabad Fort in Delhi), so the emperor probably did seek Lahori's advice.

The names of two other architects, Mir Abd al-Karim and Makramat Khan, also show up in documents concerning the Taj Mahal. Although both were accomplished architects, both men are listed as supervisors, not architects, for the Taj Mahal. Shah Jahan himself was probably the chief designer of his wife's tomb.

THE BASIC DESIGN OF THE TOMB

At the north end of the complex, on the bank of the river, sits the tomb. This building is a domed structure made of white marble inlaid with colorful gemstones in the shapes of flowers. Passages from the Quran (also Koran, the holy book of the Islamic faith) are inlaid in black marble.

WAS THE TAJ MAHAL BUILT BY AN ITALIAN OR A FRENCHMAN?

In 1642 Father Sebastian Manrique, a monk traveling in India, named an Italian, Geronimo Veroneo, as the architect of the Taj Mahal. Manrique wrote that "the emperor summoned him and informed him that he desired to erect a great and sumptuous tomb for his dead wife, and he was required to erect a great design for this, for the Emperor's inspection."

In 1844 an Englishman toured India and wrote that "the magnificent building [the Taj Mahal] and all the palaces of Agra and Delhi were, I believe, designed by Austin de Bordeaux, a Frenchman of great talent and merit, in whose ability and integrity the Emperor placed much reliance."

For many years, European literature stated that the tomb was built by either Veroneo or by de Bordeaux. Both were European artists in the Mughal court. Based on the artists' own letters, though, historians know that neither of them built the Taj Mahal or were even trained in architecture.

Europeans couldn't believe that anything so beautiful could have been designed by a non-European. Europeans of the time considered the people of India uncivilized. They recognized that the Taj Mahal was a magnificent building. So they thought it couldn't have been designed by an Indian.

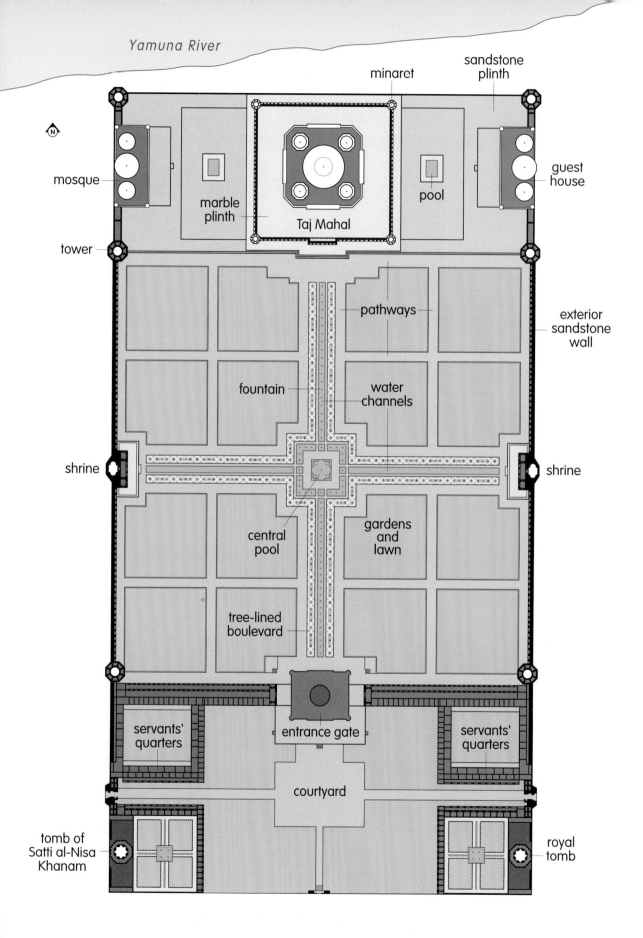

Yamuna River

minaret

sandstone plinth

N

mosque

guest house

tower

marble plinth

Taj Mahal

pool

pathways

exterior sandstone wall

fountain

water channels

shrine

shrine

central pool

gardens and lawn

tree-lined boulevard

entrance gate

servants' quarters

servants' quarters

courtyard

tomb of Satti al-Nisa Khanam

royal tomb

Above, Colorful gemstone inlays in the shapes of flowers and leaves cover much of the white marble of the tomb. *Opposite,* A site plan of the Taj Mahal complex shows the buildings, gardens, walls, and entrance gate. The white circles at the top of the plan represent the domes of buildings faced with white marble.

The tomb sits on a large marble platform, called a plinth. At each corner of the platform is a minaret (a tall, narrow tower from which a Muslim crier calls the devout to prayer). It is this building that is called the Taj Mahal, although the name often refers to the whole complex.

On the west side of the tomb is a mosque. On the east side is a guest house. The two buildings seem identical from the outside. At the southern end of the complex is an enormous entrance gate. Between the entrance gate at the south end and the buildings at the north end is a large garden. It includes open lawn, flower gardens and shade trees, a long reflecting pool with fountains, and two small shrines. The entire complex is enclosed by a red sandstone wall. A large courtyard outside the entrance gate, with more tombs and a market, serves as a gathering place for visitors.

Mughal court records refer to Mumtaz Mahal's tomb as the Illumined Tomb, probably because of the beautiful decorations and passages from the Quran inlaid in the marble. ("Illumined" refers to lustrous decoration, and marble reflects light well.) As the years passed, though, the tomb and its surrounding complex came to be called the Taj Mahal. Historians aren't really sure why, but most likely the name is an abbreviation of "Mumtaz Mahal."

THE ORIGINS OF MUGHAL ARCHITECTURE

The Taj Mahal, a spectacular example of Mughal architecture, blends Islamic, Hindu, and Persian styles. Islamic architecture features pointed arches, minarets, domes, airy interior spaces, and decorations using the natural world and geometric designs. Human or animal figures never appear in Islamic architecture because it is against Islamic beliefs. In the sixteenth century, the main examples of Islamic architecture were religious structures such as mosques or tombs.

Hindu architecture uses elaborate decorations and carvings in dark, closed interiors, and beehive-shaped exterior domes. In the sixteenth century, the main examples of Hindu architecture were also religious structures, such as temples. Because Hindus cremate their dead, they do not build tombs.

Persian architecture features *iwans* (half-domed structures), double-shelled domes (domes that are larger on the exterior than the interior), brightly glazed brickwork, and colorful inlaid mosaics. Persian buildings were often surrounded by beautiful gardens. In the sixteenth century, Persia (present-day Iran) was famous for its skilled architects, engineers, and garden designers.

The Mughals took elements from each of these three architectural traditions. In more than one hundred years of experimentation and refinement, they developed their own distinct architectural style. Because the Mughals were Muslims, they incorporated most of the elements of Islamic architecture into all their buildings but especially into their tombs and mosques. Because they used local Hindu craftsmen to build their structures, Mughal architecture also incorporated the elaborate carvings, decorations, and fine craftsmanship that characterized Hindu buildings. And because most of the architects and engineers employed by the Mughals were trained in Persia, Mughal architectural structures also showed a strong Persian influence, with iwans, beautiful gardens, and inlaid decorations.

Mughals made another refinement in developing their own style. They made their buildings huge and lavish. Mughal architecture was known for its grand scale.

Humayun's tomb *(above)* is constructed of red and white sandstone with inlays of yellow and black marble.

The Mughals began building almost as soon as they conquered the Ganges and Indus River Valleys in northern India. Many of the architectural features found in the Taj Mahal were first tried out in other buildings, such as the tombs of the emperors Humayun and Akbar.

HUMAYUN'S TOMB

The tombs of Humayun and Akbar were elaborate architectural experiments. Humayun's tomb, the first major tomb in Mughal style, was built by Akbar in 1562 in Delhi, India. Constructed of red and white sandstone and black and yellow marble, it sits in the middle of a large walled garden of several acres. Four channels of water, one from each side of the building, flow through gates in each of the four walls that surround the complex.

Humayun's tomb includes an iwan and a double-shelled dome. A double-shelled dome allows the inner shell, or ceiling, of the dome to be in perfect proportion to the room it covers, while the outer shell of the dome soars to a graceful height on the exterior of the building. There are also several iwans in the buildings and entrance gate of the Taj Mahal complex, and the tomb building has a double-shelled dome.

AKBAR'S TOMB

Akbar's tomb was the next major tomb built by the Mughals. The massive five-story building still sits in the middle of a 150-acre (61-hectare) garden in Sikandra, about 2.5 miles (4 km) west of Agra. It is made of red sandstone inlaid with quantities of white marble. This tomb has been compared to a pyramid, since its five stories, each smaller than the one beneath, are stacked on top of one another.

Because the building is red and lacks a dome, it doesn't resemble the Taj Mahal. Yet several architectural details from Akbar's tomb were copied in the later tomb. A row of domed kiosks (open pavilions)

Akbar's tomb is not nearly as graceful as the Taj Mahal, but some of its architectural details inspired the Taj Mahal's architect.

WHITE MARBLE AND MUGHAL RULERS

When the Mughals began building palaces and forts and tombs, white marble was reserved for the tombs of Muslim saints because it symbolized Paradise. Humayun was not a saint, so his tomb was built from red and white sandstone and black and yellow marble. Using white marble would have been an affront to Allah, the Islamic name for God.

By the time Akbar died, this practice was starting to change, probably due to the preferences of the Mughal rulers themselves rather than any change in religious attitudes. Akbar's tomb was built of red sandstone, but it was lavishly decorated with white marble. The white marble gave the emperor an association with sainthood and the Paradise of Islam.

Shah Jahan's use of white marble in the Taj Mahal was a further departure from accepted practices. He may have chosen that beautiful material as a fitting tribute to the beauty of his wife. Or he may have chosen white marble to make a connection between Mughal rule and the divine rule of Allah.

stretches across the top of Akbar's tomb, like a row of marble mushrooms. This same architectural detail shows up at the Taj Mahal, as do the rows of pointed arches found in the first level of Akbar's tomb.

Both Humayun's and Akbar's tombs took elements of Persian, Islamic, and Hindu architecture and altered and combined them into something distinctly Mughal. Both contributed to the design of the Taj Mahal.

THE FOUR-SQUARE CHARBAGH

The Mughals also adopted elaborate gardens from the Persians. Persian gardens were laid out in symmetrical patterns, with still pools and sparkling fountains. They were filled with leafy fruit trees and fragrant flowers. This style was brought to India by Babur. He was an avid gardener who considered India to be a dusty wasteland sorely in need of beautification.

When the Muslim Mughals began building large tombs, they added Persian gardens. The gardens were modified to portray Paradise, the place that receives the dead, as described in their holy scripture, the Quran. The Quran tells of a paradise containing flowers, trees, and the

Four Rivers of Paradise. Allah (the Islamic name for God) sits at the far side of the four rivers. To portray an earthly version of this Islamic ideal, Akbar developed a new garden design, the four-square charbagh.

In the four-square charbagh, two intersecting channels of water create the Four Rivers of Paradise, as well as four squares of land within it. Humayun's tomb sits right on top of the intersecting channels of the Four Rivers of Paradise.

This fanciful depiction of Akbar's tomb complex shows how the gardens were divided into four squares.

The Taj Mahal also features a four-square charbagh. One of its channels of water runs north-south, the other runs east-west. The channels intersect in the center of the complex, dividing it into four separate areas and creating four "separate" rivers. The placement of the Taj Mahal—as it relates to the Four Rivers of Paradise—has puzzled historians because it apparently sits at the far end of the four-square charbagh, at the place where the Throne of Allah should be.

When Shah Jahan designed the Taj Mahal, he took into consideration the architectural developments and refinements of his ancestors. By drawing upon everything the Mughals had developed in the last one hundred years, he intended to create the greatest tomb the world had ever seen. A magnificent tomb could never replace his beloved Mumtaz Mahal. But it would show the world the place she had held in his heart.

Chapter Three
CONSTRUCTION BEGINS

(1631–1632)

THE TAJ MAHAL COMPLEX WAS a large project, but Shah Jahan wanted it built as quickly as possible. Thousands of workers flocked to Agra. Many may have arrived as early as September 1631. At the start of construction, most of these workers provided unskilled physical labor—digging and lifting stone for the foundation.

The entire site had to be excavated to a depth of several yards. By January, in the dry season, workers labored under the broiling sun, struggling to remove yards of hard-packed

The finished tomb complex is reflected in the Yamuna River.

earth and silt from the building site. The temperature was over 100 degrees Fahrenheit (38 degrees Celsius). Workers wiped sweat from their brows and swatted at insects droning lazily in the heavy heat. Noise from traffic on the river mingled with the clanging of spades and thudding of clods of dirt.

The workers loaded the excavated dirt into carts drawn by teams of oxen and hauled it away, most likely to the outskirts of Agra. Some of the dirt may have been kept to level other areas of the site. It had not rained for two months, and clouds of dust rose in the air as the oxcarts rumbled in to deliver supplies.

DIVERTING THE MONSOON RAINS

The next step was to build the foundation for the tomb. The excavation was filled in with densely packed gravel to prevent seepage from the

Yamuna River. This step was especially critical because the tomb was so close to the river. The foundation had to be stable, or the entire structure could sink into the mud or be swept away during the floods. In June the rains brought by the winds of the monsoon season (June through October) would start again. By August the site would be soggy with rainwater, and the Yamuna River would be dangerously swollen. To divert the river water, a series of conduits, or drainage pipes, encased in stone and mortar were built into the foundation. Shafts or "wells" of ebony and mahogany wood were sunk into the conduit system to ventilate it and help keep it dry. There are rumored to be more than one thousand wells in the foundation of the Taj Mahal. About twenty walled-up subterranean chambers are also in the foundation, although their purpose (and the reason for walling them up) remains unknown.

When the conduits, ventilation system, and underground chambers were complete, workers filled in the excavated area with stone and mortar to bring it to ground level. Historian Lahori gives a poetic description of the building of the Taj Mahal's foundation, which, according to him, began in January 1632. "And when the spade-wielders with robust arms and hands strong as steel, had with unceasing effort excavated down to the water table, the ingenious masons and architects of astonishing achievements most firmly built the foundation with stone and mortar up to the level of the ground."

> "And when the spade-wielders with robust arms and hands strong as steel, had with unceasing effort excavated down to the water table, the ingenious masons and architects of astonishing achievements most firmly built the foundation with stone and mortar up to the level of the ground."
>
> –Lahori

MUMTAZABAD

Once construction was under way, there were probably about five thousand workers at the site every day. Some workers already lived in Agra, but many came from other parts of the Mughal Empire. Most brought their families with them because the Taj Mahal was going to take many years to complete. Agra was a bustling capital city, and there was sure to be more work when the project was completed.

Most of the workers settled in the nearby town of Mumtazabad. This was not a squalid, temporary construction camp. Shah Jahan had deliberately included a town in his designs for the Taj Mahal complex. He intended the town to remain long after the Taj Mahal was finished.

Mumtazabad became a thriving community. Two intersecting bazaar streets formed four market areas.

AKBARABAD OR AGRA?

Mughal cities still endure, but their names have changed. Agra was called Akbarabad during the Mughal Empire. It was named after Akbar, because he chose that site along the Yamuna River to build a new capital city.

Shah Jahan grew up in Akbarabad, yet before construction on the Taj Mahal was finished, he founded a new capital city, Shahjahanabad, later called Delhi. (Not far from Delhi is New Delhi, the capital of India, which was built in the twentieth century.)

The town of Mumtazabad, built to house the workers on the Taj Mahal, is called Tajganj in modern times. It has apartment buildings and a thriving marketplace, bustling with tourists buying food, souvenirs, and other wares.

Crowded bazaars similar to this one helped make Mumtazabad a thriving community.

South of this area was another square and two more market areas. The markets were lined with rows of stalls where vendors sold their wares. Rows of apartment buildings and small houses were built around the bazaars. Women shopped and chatted, while children played in the street and splashed in the river. Merchants called out to entice people to buy their wares. Above the sound of laughter and village life, the noise of construction clanged and rumbled in the air.

The red sandstone plinth was built under the tomb, guest house, and mosque complex.

THE PLINTH FOR THE MAUSOLEUM, MOSQUE, AND GUEST HOUSE

When the foundation was finished, workers started on the main plinth. A plinth is a large stone base on which a group of buildings sits. The tomb, mosque, and guest house would sit on the main plinth, which was approximately 208 yards (190 m) long, 78 yards (71 m) wide, and 9 yards (8 m) high.

Unskilled laborers built the main plinth by hefting stones into place and securing them with mortar. Skilled laborers then attached slabs of red sandstone to the stone with iron dowels and clamps. The facing stone was measured and cut with utmost precision.

THE FIRST URS

The first plinth was probably finished when the first *urs*—a ceremony held to mark the anniversary of someone's death—for Mumtaz Mahal was held at the site in June 1632. Thousands of people—nobles, scholars, holy men, rich and poor alike—attended the event. Shah Jahan invited everyone. Enormous tents and canopies were put up in the courtyard of the complex, and luxurious carpets covered the ground. Several tents probably sat on the newly built plinth. Throughout the night and the next day, holy men recited verses from the Quran and prayed for Mumtaz Mahal.

> Slabs of sandstone were "so smoothly cut and joined by expert craftsmanship that even close inspection fails to reveal any cracks between them. . . . "
>
> **—Lahori**

A lavish feast was served first to the men who attended. Women were served separately later. Fifty thousand rupees were distributed to the poor. A rupee is an Indian unit of money, worth approximately fifteen cents in modern times. During Shah Jahan's time, it was worth a great deal more. Distributing fifty thousand rupees was probably equivalent to distributing ten thousand dollars.

For several days, the atmosphere around the Taj Mahal resembled that of a festive bazaar. Construction halted during the urs but resumed as soon as it was over. The next part of construction was the tomb itself.

ROYAL WOMEN AND TOMBS

The Taj Mahal was the most glorious tomb the Mughals ever built. It was also the first major tomb built for a woman. Tombs had been built for royal women, but they were usually not as grand as the ones built for royal men. A royal wife was usually buried with her husband in a tomb designed and built for him. Shah Jahan ended up being buried next to Mumtaz Mahal. But the Taj Mahal tomb was originally built just for her.

Chapter Four
BRICKS AND WHITE MARBLE
(1632–1637)

Above, White marble faces the tomb and the minarets. *Opposite,* Donkeys and oxen hauled construction supplies by land, and boats delivered them to the river side of the tomb complex.

FOR NEARLY A YEAR, A FLURRY of activity and noise had swirled around the site of the Taj Mahal. Carts rumbled back and forth daily along the main roads of Agra delivering loads of bricks, marble, and red sandstone. Boats carried other supplies up the Yamuna River. Month by month, the population of Mumtazabad grew as more and more workers arrived.

Despite the constant activity, there was very little to see beyond the mounting piles of materials. In the first year, a lot of work went into things that were invisible or unremarkable. But once construction on the buildings and entrance gate started, there was something for the people of Agra to admire.

The second smaller plinth, for the tomb building, was constructed next. It was faced with white marble. The white marble plinth was approximately 67 yards (61 m) square and 4 yards (4 m) high.

HOW THE TAJ MAHAL STAYS UP

Shah Jahan designed the buildings and gardens of the Taj Mahal complex to complement each other and to frame Mumtaz Mahal's tomb, the highlight of the complex. The two-story octagonal (eight-sided) tomb building has twenty-eight iwans, or half-domed structures. A large dome, flanked by four smaller domes—one near each corner—would cover the roof.

Iwans are soaring and beautiful, but they also serve a practical purpose. When weight presses down on an arched shape, it doesn't press in a straight line, or in only one place. It presses in a downward curve along the sides of the arch and into the foundation. Because the weight is distributed over a wider area, arches can usually hold more weight than a straight wall. The Taj Mahal was going to be very heavy and the arched-domed shape of the iwans would help distribute the weight of the building into the sturdy foundation.

سـال باکبکزه وفصیل وسنک انداز باتمام مخلص حقیقت پوند قاسم خان میربر وحبـه فرنـح

وفیروزی صورت ونقش اختتام کرفت

This Mughal miniature painting depicts workers making bricks while construction goes on around them.

MILLIONS OF BRICKS

Unskilled laborers and skilled stonemasons were still needed at the complex, but skilled bricklayers were added to the payroll. Bricklayers were important because the Taj Mahal was first constructed from brick, then faced with white marble.

The scaffolding was also made of brick. Scaffolding is a temporary framework for workers to stand on to reach the upper levels of a building. During the 1600s, scaffolding was usually constructed from bamboo and wood. It was a relatively simple part of any building project. No one knows why the scaffolding for the Taj Mahal was made of brick. Erecting it must have been almost as big a project as making the building itself.

Mir Abd al-Karim and Makramat Khan, the chief supervisors, were at the site every day. Workers were divided into teams, depending on their skill levels or what needed to be done. Each team had a supervisor, who reported directly to Mir Abd al-Karim or Makramat Khan. Supervisors shouted out orders as workers scurried around the building, mixing mortar, stacking bricks, and working on the scaffolding.

Every work team probably had bricklayers. They would have been needed to work on scaffolding, wall, and iwan construction. Engineers and architects were also always present, measuring and making sure that plans were being accurately reproduced. On the riverbank and at the south end of the complex—where the entrance gate would be—other supervisors checked in supplies as they arrived and directed carts and laborers to their proper places.

A RAMP FOR WHITE MARBLE

Workers probably built the first story of the tomb, its four central iwans, and the scaffolding at the same time. The project required millions of bricks and vast quantities of white marble. As soon as the bricklayers finished a portion of the building, it was faced with the special white marble that came from the quarries of Makrana, about 200 miles (320 km) away, just southwest of present-day Jaipur.

The giant blocks of marble far outweighed a cartload of bricks. Some weighed as much as 6 tons (6 metric tons). The marble was delivered in wagons drawn by teams of twenty oxen or several elephants. To transport marble to the site, a 10-mile-long (16-km) ramp of tamped-down dirt was built through Agra. Its gradual incline reached up the side of the tomb. Animals pulled heavy carts directly to the upper portions of the building. A system of pulleys lifted the supplies ever farther.

The slabs of marble were cut to the correct dimensions at the quarry, but stonecutters smoothed and polished the marble at the site. The

BEAMS AND PULLEYS

Post-and-beam pulley systems were used to get large blocks of marble to the uppermost parts of a building. At the Taj Mahal tomb, teams of oxen carried heavy materials as far as they could up the dirt ramp. Then workers tied ropes around the materials, such as the blocks of marble, making sure they were securely fastened. The ropes were run through a series of pulleys that extended from beams at the top of the structure.

The workers attached the loose end of the rope to two elephants or a team of oxen on the ground. The animals were then driven forward. The wheels in the pulley system transferred the weight of the marble across the whole system and allowed the ropes to move smoothly. As the animals walked forward, the block of marble was slowly hoisted into position.

finished marble slabs were then attached to the brick structure with iron clamps and dowels.

MARBLE, MARBLE . . . MORE MARBLE!

Thousands of documents—daily pay slips, orders and payment for mortar, bricks, marble, and gemstones—must have been created during the construction of the Taj Mahal. But only four documents are known to still exist. All four of these documents involve Raja Jai Singh, the person who provided the land for the Taj Mahal. Three of the four documents direct him to ship marble to Agra without delay.

Raja Jai Singh was clearly a well-to-do nobleman, powerful in his own right. He may have owned a quarry in Makrana, or he may have had a building project of his own that required marble from Makrana. Wealthy and powerful as he was, he still must have been uncomfortable when he received a note from the emperor's administrators in September 1632. It stated:

We hereby order that, whatever the number of stone-cutters and carts-on-hire for loading the stone that may be required . . . the Raja should make them available to him; and the wages of the stone-cutters and the rent-money of the carts, he will provide with funds from the royal treasurer . . . and he should consider this a matter of utmost importance, and not deviate from this order.

> "We hereby order that, whatever the number of stone-cutters and carts-on-hire for loading the stone that may be required . . . the Raja should make them available to him. . . ."
>
> **–a letter to Raja Jai Singh**

In February 1633, a second note again directed Raja Jai Singh to ship the marble quickly. And in June 1637, when construction on the interior of the tomb was at its peak, another note was sent to him.

Raja Jai Singh's agents may have been quarrying marble, for the note urges Raja Jai Singh to "strongly impress upon his people that by no means are they to muster stone-cutters . . . and whatever stone-cutters are available should be sent to the royal agents at Makrana. And regarding strict compliance as necessary in the matter, he should not disobey or deviate from this order, and should consider it his responsibility."

A DOUBLE-SHELLED DOME

The most spectacular part of Mumtaz Mahal's tomb was the enormous white marble dome crowning it. The dome would be similar to the one on Humayun's tomb, only larger and more impressive. In addition to the main dome, four smaller domes would flank it—one on each corner of the building.

The Taj Mahal's domes were constructed after the first and second stories of the building were complete. The main dome sits in the exact center of the building and rises to 144 feet (44 m). The dome is double-shell, one size on the interior and another size on the exterior, a design that Mughal architects chose to give a building perfect visual balance.

The Taj Mahal's main dome is huge on the outside. But a dome that large would have overwhelmed the central interior chamber of the building. So a vaulted ceiling, or false dome, was constructed on the inside. The central chamber is still domed, but its dome is smaller and in proportion to the interior space.

An enormous white marble dome crowns the tomb. It is flanked by four smaller domes, one of which can be seen in this photograph. One of the four minarets (right) is also visible.

All domes are very heavy. The distribution of a dome's weight, though, is similar to that of an arch. The weight starts at the top of the dome, then moves downward and outward over the surface. The weight of the Taj Mahal's dome spreads out over the dome itself into the building on which it rests, and from there, the iwans and arches in the structure transmit the weight down into the plinths and foundation.

The inner dome of a double-shelled dome only supports its own weight. It doesn't support any weight from the exterior dome. In the Taj Mahal, the weight of the inner dome transmits downward into arches and iwans in the interior of the building and into the plinths and foundation.

THE INTERIOR OF THE TOMB

Shah Jahan designed Mumtaz Mahal's tomb as a public shrine to be visited by all members of society. So the interior needed to be as impressive as the exterior. The central chamber of the building, beneath the main dome, held the cenotaph (monument tomb) of the queen. On each of the two stories, four large rooms radiate from the central domed area. Four octagonal rooms on each story flank the four corners. Altogether sixteen rooms (eight on each level) surround the central chamber. These rooms also contain arches, which help support the weight of the building. Like the exterior, the interior of the building is faced with white marble, much of it elaborately carved and decorated.

Construction on the tomb building was probably finished around 1637, but the tomb was only a portion of the complex. A mosque, guest house, massive entrance gate, and high sandstone wall to enclose the complex were also under construction.

SCAFFOLDING: FIVE YEARS OR OVERNIGHT?

Scaffolding is usually designed to be taken apart quickly. It's not supposed to be permanent. But when the Taj Mahal tomb building was finished, the construction supervisors told Shah Jahan that its brick scaffolding was so sturdy that it would take five years to take apart.

This was unacceptable to Shah Jahan. He thought about it, then announced that anyone who helped take down the scaffolding could keep the bricks. Since bricks were an expensive and desirable building material, Shah Jahan hoped this incentive would speed up the process. It is said that the scaffolding surrounding the Taj Mahal disappeared overnight.

Taj Mahal Exterior and Double-Shelled Dome

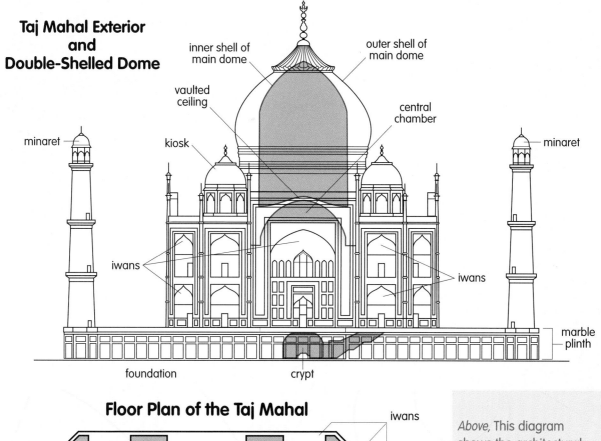

inner shell of main dome

outer shell of main dome

vaulted ceiling

central chamber

minaret

kiosk

minaret

iwans

iwans

marble plinth

foundation

crypt

Floor Plan of the Taj Mahal

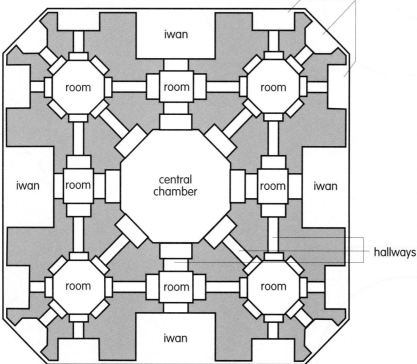

iwans

iwan

room

room

room

iwan

room

central chamber

room

iwan

room

room

room

iwan

hallways

Above, This diagram shows the architectural elements visible on the Taj Mahal. The interior spaces of the double-shelled dome, the ceiling of the central chamber, and the crypt holding the actual bodies of Mumtaz and Shah Jahan are depicted in grey. *Left,* The floor plan of one of the levels of the tomb building shows the symmetry of the building. The cenotaph (monument tomb) lies in the central room.

Chapter Five
THE ILLUMINED TOMB
(1632–1643)

BY 1637 THE CENTRAL DOME of the Taj Mahal rose skyward like a fantastic fairy castle. The white marble glowed like fire in the noonday sun and shimmered with pale shades of pink and lavender at dawn and twilight. Its beauty was reflected and doubled in the ever-changing waters of the Yamuna River smoothly flowing past.

Every year on the anniversary of Mumtaz Mahal's death, Shah Jahan commemorated her with a lavish urs held at the site. Holy men recited the Quran, thousands feasted, and money was passed out to the poor.

Shah Jahan carried on with his duties as emperor. But his wife's death affected him deeply.

"He did not for long years derive any enjoyment from colorful clothes, dresses, songs, scents of new invention," court historian Salih reported, "and during... ceremonies, and other times, tears would involuntarily flow from his august eyes."

In 1638, seven years after Mumtaz Mahal's death, Shah Jahan decided to build a new city in present-day Delhi. Perhaps he found Agra depressing without Mumtaz

Above, A portrait of Mumtaz Mahal. Muslim rulers often ignored the Islamic law against depicting humans, and their books were lavishly illustrated. *Opposite,* Mumtaz Mahal's tomb is framed by the arch of the entrance gate in the southern wall.

Mahal. Or perhaps he just decided he wanted a new residence. Whatever his reasons, starting in 1638, he rarely stayed in Agra. He spent much of his time overseeing the construction of Shahjahanabad, as the new city was called.

THE MOSQUE AND GUEST HOUSE

The tomb building was most likely completed in 1638 or 1639. The mosque, guest house, and entrance gate would have been well under way by that time too.

According to Islamic law, tombs must be accompanied by a place to pray, so a mosque was built about 80 feet (24 m) to the west of the Taj Mahal. The red sandstone that covered the brick construction held decorative inlays of white marble and colored stones laid out in floral patterns.

Three domes—a central dome flanked by two smaller domes—top the mosque. A domed kiosk rests on each corner of the building. Visitors enter the light, airy interior through a large iwan in the center of the facade.

An identical building east of the Taj Mahal, referred to as the guest house, looks exactly like the mosque from the outside. Inside, however, it is slightly different.

Both the mosque and guest house are much smaller than the tomb building. But both buildings are in perfect proportion to it. The tops of their central domes reach exactly to the middle of the Taj Mahal's great dome. No matter how lovely anything else in the complex is, its scale is smaller and its decorations less ornate. The tomb was what mattered, and nothing was permitted to interfere with its importance.

THE MINARETS OF THE TAJ MAHAL

The last things built at the north end of the complex were four white marble minarets, one on each corner of the white marble plinth of the tomb building. Minarets are tall towers, usually located next to a mosque. The Muslim crier climbs the staircase inside the tower and calls the Muslim faithful to prayers from the top.

The Taj Mahal's mosque needed only one minaret, but Shah Jahan built four to keep the layout of the tomb perfectly symmetrical. The minarets were built to lean slightly away from the tomb. This was done so that if they ever collapsed, they would fall away from the tomb and not damage it.

THE GATE OF THE TAJ MAHAL

A massive red sandstone gate forms the southern entrance to the Taj Mahal complex. This gate and the forecourt in front of it were designed to be a transition zone between the bustling world of Mumtazabad and the serenity of the tomb complex.

The main gate looks more like a building than a gate. It is taller than a modern four-story apartment building. A tall tower topped with a domed kiosk

The entrance gate is a spectacular piece of architecture, too. It is inlaid with white and black marble and semi-precious stones and is topped by a series of domed kiosks.

stands at each corner of the gate. Marching across the top of the gate are eleven small domed kiosks, exactly like those found on Akbar's tomb. The gate is inlaid with white marble, calligraphic verses from the Quran, and floral designs of precious stones. The doors are made of precious metals.

Visitors entered through an enormous entry iwan in the center of the gate. From the outside, the gate is so large that it blocks the Taj Mahal from view. As visitors pass through the gate, they see the Taj Mahal shimmering like a jewel in the distance, framed by the entry iwan. Shah Jahan and his guests did not use this main gate. They entered the Taj Mahal complex at the north end by way of the river.

INLAY AND CARVING

From a distance, the Taj Mahal looks white. Up close the visitor sees that the interior and exterior surfaces of the building are covered with complex floral patterns inlaid with brilliant semiprecious stones and flowers carved into the marble. The technique of inlaying precious stones into stone is known in Arabic as *parchin kari.*

The parchin kari inlay is formed of semiprecious stones in floral designs set into the marble.

ARTISTS AND THE MUGHAL COURT

The Mughals were known for their great wealth and love of jewels and finery. Starting with Akbar, the Mughal court sponsored a great artistic community—painters, poets, jewelers, stonecutters, and fine metalworkers. Many of these artists came from Europe.

Emperors used the artists to record court life through painting and poetry and to create jewelry for members of the court. More than just an amateur architect and collector of jewels, Shah Jahan was extremely knowledgeable in both areas and probably knew how to cut and set gemstones himself. Under Shah Jahan, Mughal artistic achievements reached new heights, as the Taj Mahal shows.

Shah Jahan is depicted in this lavishly illustrated Mughal miniature painting. Mughal arts flourished under his rule.

Flowers were also carved in patterns directly on the walls with a technique known as *manabbat kari*.

To create the parchin kari inlays, artists drew the patterns on the marble with henna, a red dye. Then they chiseled out the designs. Next they cut the stones to fit the design and inserted them. Parchin kari flowers are found in abundance on the tomb, mosque, guest house, and gate of the complex. In Islamic culture, flowers symbolize Paradise and the kingdom of Allah. Mumtaz Mahal's tomb complex was intended to represent this paradise—on earth.

Forty-three different types of gems decorate the Taj Mahal. Turquoise came from Tibet, crystal and jade came from China, and lapis lazuli came from Afghanistan. Coral, agate, jasper, amethyst, malachite—nothing was too fine for Mumtaz Mahal's tomb.

A carving that stands out from a flat surface is produced through a technique called manabbat kari. Parchin kari is found throughout the complex, while the manabbat kari is found primarily on the interior of the tomb. Artists drew the manabbat kari flowers directly on the marble with henna, then they carved them out of the marble with an assortment of fine chisels.

CALLIGRAPHY

Twenty-two passages and fourteen entire chapters from the Quran, written in calligraphy, are inlaid in black marble around the iwans. Inlaid calligraphy also appears on the main gate, mosque, and guest house. All verses are in Arabic, the language of the Quran.

Most of the calligraphy was done while the buildings were under construction. From 1632 through 1637, one man, Amanat Khan, spent all his waking hours working on the inlaid Quran verses. He was the official calligrapher for the Taj Mahal complex.

Amanat Khan was renowned throughout the Mughal Empire. A native of Shiraz, Persia, he came to India around 1608. Shortly after his arrival, Jahangir appointed him to design the calligraphy for the tomb of Akbar. From then on, Amanat Khan appears to have held several trusted positions within the government, including acting as an escort for the Persian ambassador.

The honorary title, Amanat Khan, means "Lord of Trust." It was conferred upon him in June 1632, one year after Mumtaz Mahal's death. Before that he was known as Abd al-Haqq. Shah Jahan probably awarded the title to him in recognition of the work he had already done on the tomb.

To inlay the calligraphic inscriptions, Amanat Khan first worked out the design in his studio. Then he drew the design on the building's marble and chiseled it out. He placed the black marble inlays in the chiseled-out areas.

THE TROMPE L'OEIL OF THE TAJ MAHAL

Amanat Khan used an optical trick to inlay the Quranic verses on the Taj Mahal. The letters appear to be equally sized, but they're not. As the letters move upward to the peak of any arch, they gradually get bigger.

This *trompe l'oeil* (French for "trick the eye") compensates for how the human eye sees distance. Things that are far away look smaller than things that are close. By varying the size of the letters, the inscriptions look perfectly proportioned no matter where you stand.

Passages from the Quran, inlaid in black marble, can be found in the tomb, the mosque, the guest house, and on the main gate.

Usually a holy man chose the Quranic verses to be used on a tomb. The artist then executed whatever the holy man chose. But Amanat Khan, well versed in the Quran, was almost a learned holy man himself. He was also a trusted noble and member of the Mughal court. Many historians believe that Amanat Khan may have been responsible for both choosing and executing the Quranic verses at the Taj Mahal.

Shah Jahan thought so highly of Amanat Khan that the calligrapher was the only person allowed to sign his name on the tomb. He signed the tomb twice and dated each signature. These dates suggest that the tomb building—or at least the calligraphy—was entirely finished by 1638 or 1639.

All this construction and embellishment cost money, lots of it. From 1632 through 1640, the expense to the Mughal treasury was staggering. Court historians record that the buildings in the complex cost five million rupees. This amount did not include the gardens. With the buildings in the complex finished around 1640 or 1641, it was time to start work on the element that would tie everything together: the magnificent four-square charbagh gardens.

Chapter Six
THE GARDEN OF PARADISE ON EARTH
(1640–1643)

ALL THE STRUCTURES IN THE Taj Mahal complex were probably completed by 1640. Artists were still working on the parchin kari on the buildings, but the largest, noisiest parts of construction were finished. The massive brick scaffolding surrounding the tomb was gone, and the dirt ramp through Agra was shoveled away. Amanat Khan had left, and even Shah Jahan was away, supervising the construction of his new city, Shahjahanabad. Still much remained to be done. The tomb complex wouldn't

Gardens, water channels, and fountains were important parts of every Mughal emperor's tomb complex.

be complete until its garden was in place. The four-square charbagh was an essential part of any Mughal tomb.

Two marble channels filled with water and studded with fountains intersect in the middle of the complex, dividing the garden into four separate areas. Intersecting pathways divide each of these four areas into four more. A large central pool sits in the center, where the water channels intersect. This pool and the main water channel (which runs north and south between the main gate and the tomb) were designed to perfectly reflect the Taj Mahal.

If Shah Jahan's court historians ever recorded information about the garden of the Taj Mahal, the records no longer exist. No one knows what plants were in the garden or how densely the garden was planted. Accounts by visiting Europeans and records of other Mughal gardens suggest that the current green lawn and two rows of cypress trees are only a small part of what was planted there during Shah Jahan's time.

SUPPLYING THE FOUR RIVERS OF PARADISE

Water was an integral part of any Mughal garden. The first thing workers did was construct the system that would deliver water to the complex, much the way modern people install sprinkler systems in their lawns before planting them. The water for the Taj Mahal's garden came from the Yamuna River. Most of the water system for the Taj Mahal lies to the west of the complex. Within the complex, the system is primarily underground.

A system of *purs*—buckets and ropes pulled by oxen or other animals—drew water from the river. The water was dumped into a broad channel, where it ended up in a huge oblong storage tank. From there another system of purs raised the water again into a large overhead water channel supported by massive arches. This overhead channel carried the water to yet another, even larger, storage tank.

Another series of fourteen purs raised the water again and dumped it into a channel that filled three large storage tanks. The last storage tank had pipes in its eastern wall. These pipes descended from the tank, went underground, and entered the Taj Mahal complex. One pipe ran toward the mosque and supplied the fountains just in front of the Taj Mahal. Other pipes supplied the north-south water channel and its pools. The water system was built so well that it has survived the centuries virtually intact.

Water was raised from the river by a series of purs—buckets attached to ropes pulled by oxen—into higher and higher storage tanks. Then the water ran down into the tomb complex to supply the channels and fountains.

The Water System of the Taj Mahal

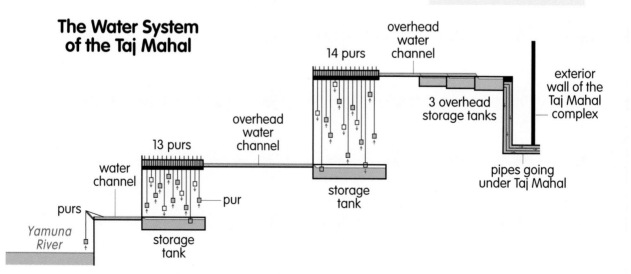

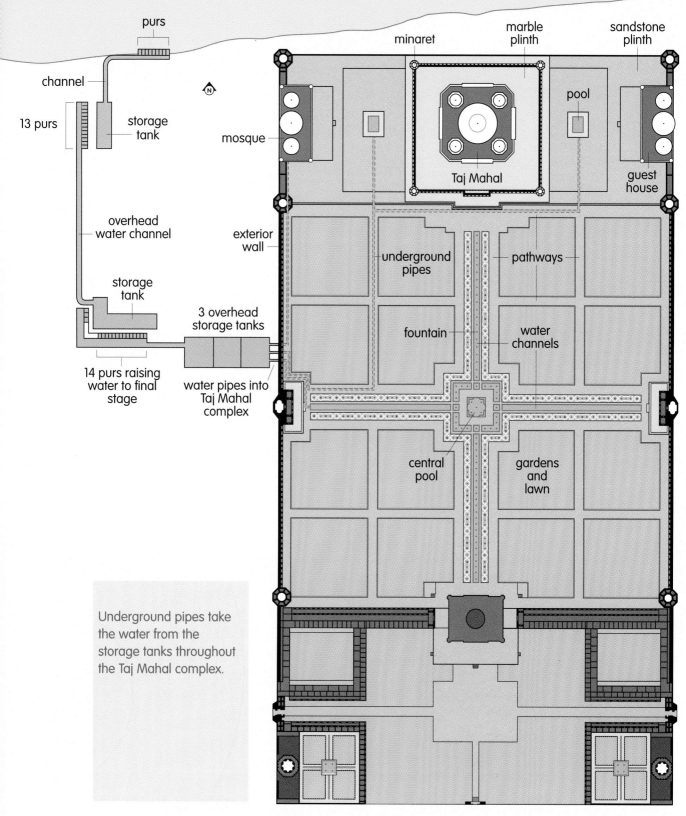

Yamuna River

purs

channel

13 purs

storage tank

overhead water channel

storage tank

14 purs raising water to final stage

3 overhead storage tanks

water pipes into Taj Mahal complex

minaret

marble plinth

sandstone plinth

mosque

pool

Taj Mahal

guest house

exterior wall

underground pipes

pathways

fountain

water channels

central pool

gardens and lawn

Underground pipes take the water from the storage tanks throughout the Taj Mahal complex.

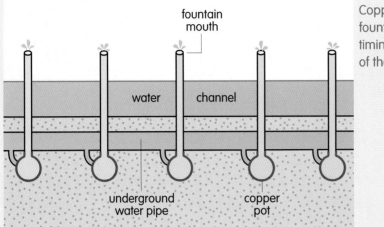

fountain mouth

water channel

Copper pots under the fountains control the timing of the release of the water.

underground water pipe

copper pot

SPARKLING FOUNTAINS

Water flowed downward from the elevated tanks and pipes of the water system to the fountains. To ensure uniform water pressure, the water supply was connected to a copper pot beneath each fountain. When all the pots were full, all the fountains went off simultaneously. The person who designed the water system for the Taj Mahal was so confident it would never need repairs that he buried the main pipe in masonry 5 feet (1.5 m) beneath a paved walkway.

THE THRONE OF GOD?

The placement of the Taj Mahal's tomb building has puzzled many historians because Mughal tombs were usually placed in the center of a four-square garden plan. In the Islamic version of paradise, the Throne of Allah was at the far end of the garden. One had to walk through all of Paradise before reaching the throne.

Based on this, the Taj Mahal's tomb building should be sitting where the central pool is, right at the intersection of the two channels of water. But the tomb building sits where the Throne of Allah should be. Historian Elizabeth Moynihan calls this effect "very un-Mughal." This break in tradition has led some historians to wonder whether Shah Jahan intended the tomb to be for himself as well as Mumtaz Mahal. Was the tomb placed at the end of the complex, instead of at the intersection, to resemble the Throne of Allah and remind people of Shah Jahan's importance?

RIVER GARDENS

Babur, the first Mughal emperor, loved gardens, and his first garden was built on the banks of the Yamuna. Although no records of the layout exist, Babur recorded its construction in his memoirs.

"The beginning was made with the large well from which water comes . . . plots of garden were seen laid out with order and symmetry, with suitable borders and parterres [ornamental gardens] in every corner, and in every border rose and narcissus in perfect arrangement."

Others followed Babur's example, and elaborate river gardens sprang up on the banks of the Yamuna. Tons of earth, rock, stone, and brick and engineering skill were employed in the construction of pavilions, terraces, pools, pathways, and water systems. Workers built sturdy landings for boats and high retaining walls to repel the Yamuna during the rainy season.

In present times, these gardens exist only in paintings from the era. But the remains of their stone walls can still be seen along the Yamuna River as it winds through Agra.

The emperor Babur loved gardens and had many constructed during his reign. In this miniature painting, he watches his gardeners measure out flower beds.

THE MISSING HALF

The 1990s brought another answer to the puzzle of the placement of Mumtaz Mahal's tomb. On the north bank of the Yamuna River, directly across from the Taj Mahal, a solitary domed tower and the remains of a red sandstone wall look out over the sluggish river. A dusty field sprawls northward from the tower, overgrown with weeds and a few scraggly trees.

Mughal documents say little of the field and its ruins. Babur was known to have had a garden on the north bank of the Yamuna, close to the site. For centuries the field was rumored to be the place where Shah Jahan started construction on his own tomb, the Black Taj, only to abandon it shortly afterward.

In the 1990s, the Archaeological Survey of India (ASI) and other international institutions launched an extensive survey of the site. In 1993 the ASI began to excavate there. The ASI archaeologists discovered that the ragged field and its crumbling structures were originally the Mahtab Garden, part of the Taj Mahal.

This ruined sandstone wall (right) faces the Taj Mahal across the Yamuna River.

Only one written reference to the Mahtab Garden survives. On December 9, 1652, Aurangzeb (Shah Jahan and Mumtaz Mahal's fifth child and third son) wrote a letter to his father when he passed through Agra after a military campaign. In it he detailed some maintenance problems with the Taj Mahal and, he wrote: "The Mahtab Garden was completely inundated, and therefore has lost its charm, but soon it will regain its verdancy. The octagonal pool and the pavilion around it are in splendid condition."

Survey measurements and satellite photos confirm that the borders of the Mahtab Garden line up exactly with the Taj Mahal complex on the other side of the river. The site's central water channel, which runs north-south, lines up perfectly with the Taj Mahal's central water channel. Before the excavation, the Mahtab channel had not been visible. It was buried under 2 to 3 yards (2 to 3 m) of dirt. Elizabeth Moynihan, one of the survey participants, points out that the main channels in the two gardens provide one long north-south axis. The Yamuna River, which runs east-west, intersects them. When reflected in the river, the Taj Mahal tomb appears to be situated at the crossing of an enormous Four Rivers of Paradise, with the Yamuna River as the east-west channel. By using the

THE MYTH OF THE BLACK TAJ

In 1676 Jean-Baptiste Tavernier, a French jewel merchant who had journeyed to India in the 1640s, wrote, "Shah Jahan began to build his own tomb on the other side of the river, but the war which he had with his sons interrupted his plan" He was referring to a rebellion by Shah Jahan's son Aurangzeb, which ended with Shah Jahan's imprisonment by his own son.

From this the story grew that the Shah Jahan's tomb was to have been black marble and linked to the Taj Mahal by a bridge over the Yamuna River. For centuries guidebooks for the Taj Mahal have routinely included this story as the explanation for the odd ruins across the river—calling them the remains of the foundation of Shah Jahan's own Black Taj, started but never completed.

With Shah Jahan imprisoned, the original purpose and beauty of the Mahtab Garden quickly vanished from memory. So when Tavernier wrote his piece on the Taj Mahal, thirty-three years after its completion, the Mahtab Garden was probably already falling into ruin. Floodwaters had probably swept away the boat landing. Only the tower and the large flat terrace by the river remained to further the myth of the Black Taj.

Yamuna as part of the Rivers of Paradise, Shah Jahan created the most opulent tomb and four-square charbagh the world had ever seen.

THE MAHTAB GARDEN

The ASI also attempted to discover what plants grew in the gardens during the time of Shah Jahan. The task was difficult because historical records show that the site had been flooded at least once in the past.

During the excavation, it became obvious that the Mahtab Garden had been flooded several times in the last 350 years—several yards of silt covered the original site. Most of the plants growing there were common weeds or plants from seeds that had washed onto the site during times of flood. But several yards down, the ASI archaeologists discovered the remains of six different species from Mughal times.

Based on the layout of the garden and the plant species discovered, the ASI was able to determine

A view of the Taj Mahal from across the Yamuna River at the site of the Mahtab Garden. In the late 1990s, researchers replanted the area to recreate the garden as it may have appeard during Shah Jahan's time.

that the Mahtab Garden was a Moonlight Garden—a garden visited primarily at night. Its walkways were plastered white for better visibility and many of its plants bloomed only at night. It was a nighttime pleasure garden designed for viewing the Taj Mahal.

The Mahtab Garden was approached by boat. There was a broad stone landing at river level and a red sandstone wall around the complex, with a domed tower on each of the four corners. From the landing, visitors climbed a flight of steps to reach the garden level.

The first thing visitors saw upon entering the garden was a large octagonal pool in the middle of a large terrace. By daylight or moonlight, the pool reflected the Taj Mahal in its clear, still waters. There was at least one pavilion on the north side of the river terrace, with a smaller pool for lotus blossoms behind it. From the center of the lotus pool, a

A princess and her court go about their evening activities in a glowing moonlight garden in this miniature painting.

THE REFLECTION OF THE TAJ MAHAL . . . AGAIN

In the 1990s, the Supreme Court of India decreed that a green belt was to be established around the Taj Mahal. So the Horticultural Department of the Archaeological Survey of India planted seven thousand saplings in the Mahtab Garden in 1998 and 1999.

An irrigation system installed to water the trees provided the Mahtab Garden with water for the first time in several hundred years. The ASI team tapped into the irrigation system and filled the pool to test their theory that the octagonal pool had been designed to reflect the Taj Mahal.

As Elizabeth Moynihan, one of the team members, reported, "By the light of a full moon on October 24, 1999, the Taj was reflected once again in the great pool of the Mahtab [Garden]. In the stillness of the night, bathed in moonlight, the glory of the garden could be imagined."

central water channel ran straight back to the north wall of the garden—a continuation of the north-south water channel at the Taj Mahal across the river.

Halfway back into the garden, the main water channel intersected another water channel that ran east-west. These two intersecting channels formed a perfect four-square charbagh in the Moonlight Garden. The Mahtab Garden also had its own water delivery system, similar to the one designed for the tomb gardens. Remains of this system can still be seen, although it is badly deteriorated.

COMPLETION OF THE TAJ MAHAL

In 1642 gardeners would have been furiously at work on the tomb gardens and moonlight gardens of the Taj Mahal. Fruit trees and beds of flowers were planted throughout the tomb garden. Flowering shrubs and bulbs lined the paved pathways. Across the river, the moonlight garden was planted with red cedars, sweet-scented jasmine, and other fragrant plants. The finishing touches were added to its pathways and pavilions.

Very few writings exist that describe the gardens of the Taj Mahal. One by François Bernier, a noted French physician who visited Agra in July

The completed Taj Mahal stands majestically above the Yamuna River.

1663, described the paths of the Taj Mahal as "raised about eight French feet above the garden [with] several garden walks covered with trees and many parterres [ornamental gardens] full of flowers."

In 1643 Shah Jahan prepared to leave Shahjahanabad and return to Agra. It was the twelfth anniversary of Mumtaz Mahal's death, and an urs would be celebrated in her honor. Only this year, everything was finally finished.

Chapter Seven
FALL OF THE MUGHALS
(1643–present)

THE TAJ MAHAL COMPLEX WAS ornate, bejeweled, and luxurious. Gemstones glistened in the iridescent white marble. The black marble verses from the Quran stood out in sharp contrast. The warm red sandstone of the outlying buildings emphasized the coolness of the white marble tomb.

With construction completed, the final touches were added, and the Taj Mahal became even more lavish. Soft Persian carpets and silk cushions, which were changed several times a week, covered the floor of the central chamber. Gates of solid silver guarded the entrance. Gold lamps and silver candlesticks decorated the walls. A door carved from a solid

Above, Mumtaz Mahal's cenotaph is decorated with flower inlays and calligraphic designs. *Opposite,* Shah Jahan returned to Agra in a royal procession like this one to celebrate the urs festival commemorating the twelfth anniversary of his wife's death.

piece of jasper opened into one of the inner passageways. Delicate incense perfumed the air, and musicians played almost continuously in the central chamber.

Mumtaz Mahal's cenotaph, her monument tomb, stood in the middle of the central chamber, directly beneath the main dome. Shah Jahan had a sheet of pearls spread over it and a gold screen placed around it. He chose his finest diamonds to lay on top. Holy men were sent to the Taj Mahal to pray beside the monument, and two thousand soldiers guarded the complex.

The urs festival commemorating the twelfth anniversary of Mumtaz Mahal's death was held on February 6, 1643, nearly five months earlier than the actual anniversary of her death. This may have been to mark the completion of the entire complex. According to the court historian Salih, "The august person of His Majesty also blessed that assembly with the light of his presence; and through recitation of prayers . . . there was achieved the means for the repose of the soul of that one . . . residing in the gardens of Paradise."

MONEY AND MAINTENANCE

Shah Jahan spent his evenings in Agra at the Mahtab Garden. The royal barge floated the short distance down from the Red Fort and tied up at the landing. The emperor, his attendants, and guests mounted the stairs to the terrace and spent the evening in luxurious splendor.

From the terrace, Shah Jahan could contemplate the Taj Mahal shining in the moonlight, its perfection reflected in the large octagonal pool. The scent of flowers wafted through the air, and fountains splashed in the background. As one historian points out, "Here in his earthly paradise he could enjoy the pleasure of sorrow."

> "Here in his earthly paradise [Shah Jahan] could enjoy the pleasure of sorrow."
>
> **–historian Elizabeth Moynihan**

When Shahjahanabad was finished in 1648, Shah Jahan moved the entire Mughal court there from Agra. The Taj Mahal was hardly abandoned, though. Most of the complex was kept in perfect condition. Documents show that Shah Jahan created a trust that received the tax revenue from thirty villages, including Mumtazabad. The large trust maintained the Taj Mahal, with money left over.

Although the Taj Mahal was a new complex of buildings, it did need maintenance. Less than ten years after its completion, it was already experiencing structural problems. Aurangzeb's December 1652 letter to his father (when he mentions the flooding of the Mahtab Garden) was to inform him that the buildings in the complex were stable but that "the dome over the blessed tomb leaks on the north side during the rainy season, and the four portals, most of the second-story alcoves, the four small domes, the four northern vestibules, and the vault of the seven-doored plinth have gotten damp."[20] He went on to add that the marble ceiling of the dome and the domes of the mosque and guest house had leaked.

Shah Jahan took care of all repairs to the tomb as long as he was emperor, and the building was well maintained. But other members of the royal family soon lost interest. Trouble was brewing on their horizon, and the Mughal Empire was beginning its decline.

IMPRISONED IN THE RED FORT

In 1657 Shah Jahan became ill. Because it appeared that he would die, three of his four sons—Dara Shikoh, Shah Shuja, and Murad Bakhsh—journeyed to see him and pay their respects. The fourth son, Aurangzeb, then a governor in the Deccan, the region where Mumtaz Mahal had died, stayed where he was.

Shah Jahan recovered. But his illness had fired Aurangzeb's ambition to become emperor. To do that, Aurangzeb would have to destroy the power of his oldest brother, Dara Shikoh, Shah Jahan's favorite son and chosen heir. Accession to the Mughal throne was often a ruthless process, and the battle Aurangzeb waged was no exception. He formed an alliance with his brother Murad Bakhsh, then marched on the forces of Dara Shikoh and crushed them. Aurangzeb then betrayed Murad Bakhsh and executed him. He chased his other brother Shah Shuja into a pirate-infested sea where he later died. He then captured Dara Shikoh, beheaded him, and sent his severed head to their father.

Aurangzeb had no qualms about killing his brothers to become emperor, but he stopped short of killing his father. He seized Shah Jahan and Jahanara, his oldest sister, and had them both imprisoned in the Red Fort in Agra. Within a year,

Prince Dara Shikoh *(center)* was Shah Jahan's favorite son and heir to his father's throne.

Shah Jahan could see the Taj Mahal from this window when he was a prisoner at the Red Fort in Agra.

Aurangzeb had eliminated all rivals, moved into the Red Fort in Shahjahanabad, and declared himself emperor.

For the next eight years, Shah Jahan was a prisoner in the Red Fort in Agra. He lived in a complex of marble apartments with silken tapestries and jeweled walls. He still had his harem, his jewels, his attendants, and almost anything he desired—except his freedom. He had always been close to his daughter Jahanara, and she remained his constant companion while they were imprisoned.

Perhaps his most treasured possession, though, was the view of the Taj Mahal. He couldn't visit it, but he could see it from his apartments in the Red Fort. He spent many hours each day gazing at the tomb of his beloved wife.

Shah Jahan's cenotaph *(left)* is next to Mumtaz Mahal's, and their bodies are both buried in the crypt below the tomb.

ANOTHER BURIAL IN THE TAJ MAHAL

In 1666 Shah Jahan became ill again. This time he did not recover. He died on January 31, 1666. Legend has it that he died gazing at a tiny mirror embedded in the wall next to his bed, tilted at an angle. From where he lay, he could see the Taj Mahal reflected in the mirror.

Jahanara wanted a royal funeral for her father, but Aurangzeb refused. Within hours of his father's death, he had the body taken by boat to the Taj Mahal. Shah Jahan was buried in a tomb under the floor of the central dome, next to Mumtaz Mahal.

It's hard to say if this arrangement was always intended or just a hasty answer of what to do with a dead ex-emperor. Shah Jahan's cenotaph in the central dome is the only element of disharmony in an otherwise perfectly symmetrical arrangement. Instead of the two cenotaphs being centered under the central dome, Mumtaz Mahal's is directly under the dome and Shah Jahan's is off to the side.

ANOTHER TOMB AT THE TAJ MAHAL

In 1647 Mumtaz Mahal's trusted friend and head lady-in-waiting, Satti al-Nisa Khanam, died. After Mumtaz Mahal's death, she had served as tutor and confidante to Princess Jahanara. A noblewoman in her own right, she was the sister of a great Persian poet and had adopted two of his daughters—one of whom married the eldest son of Amanat Khan, the calligrapher of the Taj Mahal.

Shah Jahan provided ten thousand rupees for her burial expenses. He also provided thirty thousand rupees to construct a tomb for her along the west side of the Taj Mahal complex, in the forecourt outside the main entrance gate.

CENOTAPHS VS. GRAVES

The cenotaph monuments of Mumtaz Mahal and Shah Jahan, in the central chamber of the Taj Mahal under the great dome, are not their actual coffins. Beautifully decorated and inlaid, they serve as memorials for the emperor and empress.

The bodies of Mumtaz Mahal and Shah Jahan lie in a crypt beneath the floor of the central chamber. The crypt is reached by descending a stairway in one of the side chambers on the main floor. While most of the Taj Mahal complex is open to the public, the crypt has been closed to visitors since 1991.

Yet other Mughal tombs followed this arrangement. Shah Jahan's body is to the west of Mumtaz Mahal's. Thus, as the supreme ruler, he lies closer to Mecca (the city in Saudi Arabia that is the spiritual center of Islam) than she does. Nearly thirty-five years after her death, Shah Jahan and Mumtaz Mahal were reunited under the great dome of the Taj Mahal.

END OF THE MUGHAL EMPIRE

Aurangzeb was the last of the great Mughal emperors. He took the title Alamgir (World-Shaker) and ruled with an iron fist for forty-nine years. He persecuted Hindus, reinstated a tax against non-Muslims, and alienated most groups within the empire.

He also spent vast quantities of money on fruitless military campaigns in the Deccan. The Mughal emperors had never been able to truly conquer this area. In 1682 Aurangzeb moved his court to the Deccan and established a new capital city from which to direct his military campaign. He died there, twenty-five years later, in 1707. His war in the Deccan was still unresolved, and the Mughal treasury was nearly bankrupt.

Aurangzeb's son Muazzim became the next Mughal emperor (killing two of his brothers to obtain the throne). He tried to reverse the damage his father had done, but it was too late. Hindus, Sikhs, Marathas, and other angry native people took up arms and revolted. By 1739 the Deccan was

Aurangzeb, Shah Jahan's youngest son, became emperor after him. He ruled for forty-nine years and left the Mughal treasury nearly bankrupt.

independent, and Afghanistan was a separate country. The Mughals limped along for another hundred years. One emperor after another took the throne, some reigning for only months or even weeks. In 1858 the last ruler of the Mughal Empire was exiled, not by Indians but by the British, who had an empire of their own, which included India.

The Taj Mahal had suffered throughout the fall of the Mughal Empire. Once Aurangzeb died, no family members oversaw the trust for its maintenance, and the tomb fell into disrepair. The garden of the Taj Mahal was claimed by weeds, and fallen tree limbs littered crumbling paths.

Its gold lamps, silver candlesticks, and silver doors disappeared long before the British took control—carried off by thieves and plundering chiefs. Nothing of its luxurious interior remained. During his own reign, Shah Jahan had removed the gold screen around the monument, fearing that it was too great a temptation to thieves, and replaced it with a lacy screen of cut marble.

Shah Jahan replaced the original gold screen around the cenotaph with this screen of lacy marble.

THE BRITISH EAST INDIA COMPANY

The British had been trading in India since 1613, during the reign of Jahangir. The British East India Company purchased local spices, dyes, aromatics, and cotton to ship back for sale in Europe at high prices. They stored the goods they purchased at several centers until they could be shipped to Britain. These centers, called forts, were little more than warehouses with a fence around them.

The British East India Company established trading posts like this one in various parts of India.

The first British ambassador arrived at the Mughal court in 1615. For decades the British were respectful of their hosts. Every Mughal had approved their presence in India. The British East India Company employed Indians and even trained some in the ways of European warfare. These trained men, called sepoys, learned British discipline and drilled as if they were British soldiers. Equipped with muskets and cannons, they guarded the company forts, assuring that goods being sent around the country arrived safely.

As the Mughal Empire deteriorated, the British grew bolder. Their warehouse forts became true forts. They strengthened the walls and placed cannons on the rooftops. Often this fortification was done without the consent of Indian leaders. Local resentment grew.

In 1756 the British East India Company fortified Fort William in Kolkata (Calcutta) without permission from Siraj-ud-Dawla, the local ruler. Siraj was already irritated with British tactics. He attacked Fort William, took it over, and crammed 145 British prisoners into a small cell. Most of the prisoners died of suffocation. Britain sent troops to

India. Using "the Black Hole of Calcutta" as their rallying cry, the English fought a decisive battle and took over most of the region. In 1774 Warren Hastings became the first British governor-general of the region. With a real British military presence in the country, tensions between the Indians and British increased.

In 1857 the British issued bullets to the sepoys. These bullets needed to have the cap bitten off before they would fire. A rumor quickly circulated among the sepoys that animal grease coated the bullet caps. This meant that whenever a sepoy bit off a bullet cap, he would be violating his Hindu religious beliefs against eating animals. Convinced that the British were mocking both them and their religion, the sepoys mutinied.

The Sepoy Mutiny was bloody and extensive. The sepoys were well trained and well armed. By the time the mutiny was put down in 1858, the British had also ousted the last Mughal emperor and controlled all of India as a British colony.

THE TAJ MAHAL AND THE BRITISH RAJ

The new British government in India was called the British Raj. The British did not adapt to India or incorporate its customs. Instead they adapted India to British ways. They paved streets and lined them with tall houses. Flowered curtains appeared in the windows. Parts of India began to look like London.

The British considered the native Indians primitive and backward. This contempt extended to anything native, even the magnificent

The well trained sepoy troops rebelled against the British in 1857.

English families visited the Taj Mahal and often took the jewel inlays as souvenirs.

buildings erected during the Mughal Empire. The Red Fort at Agra was used as a garrison for soldiers, and mosques were turned into government offices.

But the Taj Mahal's bejeweled surfaces still remained. The complex became a favorite picnic spot for the British. They came with chisels, and when lunch was finished, they spent the afternoon chiseling out the amethysts, jade, and other stones embedded in the building. At one point, the British even made plans to tear down the Taj Mahal and ship the pieces to Britain to be sold at auction. Wreckers had moved into the gardens and were halted only by a notification that a previous shipment of Mughal marble had failed to sell at auction in London.

The Taj Mahal might no longer exist were it not for the efforts of Lord Curzon, the British viceroy of India, appointed in 1898. He loved India and thought the Taj Mahal the most beautiful building he had ever seen. He stopped the plundering and began restoring the complex.

When Curzon left India seven years later, he called saving the Taj Mahal his greatest accomplishment. On one last visit he said, "I have written my name here, and the letters are a living joy."

THE TAJ MAHAL IN MODERN TIMES

In 1947 India gained its independence from Great Britain and established a democracy. In 1958 the government created the Archaeological Survey of India to oversee monuments of historic importance, including the Taj Mahal.

Indians are very proud of the Taj Mahal, but their country has not always had the money or other resources to maintain it properly. In 1983 the United Nations Educational, Scientific, and Cultural Organization (UNESCO) included the Taj Mahal on its World Heritage List. Because of this classification, the Taj Mahal has received significant funding from international sources. These funds help address the three biggest problems facing the Taj Mahal in modern times: damage from pollution, heavy rains, and too many visitors.

POLLUTION AND THE TAJ MAHAL

Present-day Agra is home to many coal-burning factories. The soot from these factories discolors the white marble of the Taj Mahal, turning it a grayish yellow. In addition, high concentrations of carbon monoxide in the area eat away at the marble. To prevent damage from both forms of pollution, the Taj Mahal has to be constantly cleaned. The Supreme Court of India has ruled that the coal-burning factories in Agra must either relocate or switch to cleaner-burning natural gas. The government is also taking steps to reduce other kinds of pollution in the area.

THE TAJ MAHAL DURING TIMES OF WAR

Because the Taj Mahal is India's most recognized landmark, the Indian government has taken special precautions to protect it during times of war. An enormous scaffold resembling a pile of bamboo covered the Taj Mahal during World War II (1939–1945). Any enemy aircraft flying over the Taj Mahal saw only a stockpile of bamboo. During the India–Pakistan war of 1971, the Taj Mahal was covered with green camouflage cloth, making it virtually invisible from the air. After the September 11, 2001, terrorist attacks in the United States, tensions again mounted between India and Pakistan, and in December 2001, the ASI made plans to again cover the Taj Mahal, if necessary. Ladders, ropes, and cloths were purchased. Many employees who covered the monument in 1971 still worked for the Indian government, and the ASI sought their help. Even with experienced employees, it would take fifteen to twenty days to cover the Taj Mahal.

"THE DOME OVER THE BLESSED TOMB LEAKS". . . STILL

For several months each year, India experiences heavy rains. As Aurangzeb's letter to Shah Jahan in 1652 shows, this was a problem for the Taj Mahal from the beginning. Over the centuries, water has continued to damage the tomb building and other structures. The constant humidity has corroded the iron clamps that fasten the tomb's white marble to the bricks and promotes the growth of algae and fungi.

In 1998 a three-year restoration project designed to deal with pollution and water damage was begun by a French foundation, UNESCO, and the ASI. First, chemicals were applied to two test areas, the terrace and the base of the Taj Mahal's dome, to restore the marble and prevent further deterioration. Then, both these areas were treated with a water-proofing product that also retards the growth of algae and fungi. If the products work well, the rest of the building will be treated. A conservation laboratory was established inside the Red Fort in Agra, and local scientists were sent to Europe for specialized training in the conservation and restoration of marble.

A VICTIM OF ITS OWN SUCCESS

The Taj Mahal is one of the greatest tourist attractions in the world. Each year 2.5 million people, including 900,000 foreign tourists, visit it. Shah Jahan intended the Taj Mahal to be visited and used, but not by millions

The Taj Mahal is one of the most popular tourist sites in the world.

of people. He meant it to be a place of repose and consolation. The Indian government wants people to visit and appreciate the complex, but the volume of people poses serious problems. One of the biggest hazards to the building is the humidity caused by the breath and sweat of the thousands of visitors who pass through the tomb every day.

In October 2000, the Indian government tripled the admission fee for the Taj Mahal. It hopes that the higher price will limit the number of visitors. Even if the number of visitors drops by half, the increased income will help maintain the complex.

In June 2001, the Archaeological Survey of India also formed a partnership with the Taj Group of Hotels, an association of hotels near the Taj Mahal. The hotels have agreed to donate money to the ASI to help restore the gardens (including the newly discovered Mahtab Garden), upgrade the tourist facilities, install new lighting around the monument, clean up the whole complex, and restore the pathways and fountains.

A SYMBOL FOR ETERNITY

Since 1643 the Taj Mahal has inspired awe in everyone who has seen it. After a visit to the Taj Mahal, British humorist and artist Edward Lear remarked, "Henceforth, let the inhabitants of the world be divided into two classes—them as has seen the Taj Mahal; and them as hasn't."

> "Henceforth, let the inhabitants of the world be divided into two classes—them as has seen the Taj Mahal; and them as hasn't."
> —Edward Lear

The Taj Mahal may be the most recognizable building in the world. Its soaring dome and minarets, reflected in its Four Rivers of Paradise, represent the height of architectural beauty during the reign of the Mughals. But the Taj Mahal is more than just an architectural achievement. It is a symbol of heartfelt grief and enduring love. Perhaps the Indian poet Rabindranath Tagore best described why the Taj Mahal inspires such reverence in so many: "Still one solitary tear would hang on the cheek of time, in the form of this white and gleaming Taj Mahal."

Timeline of the Mughal Empire and the Taj Mahal

1483 Babur the Tiger is born in Fergana, in Central Asia.

1526 Babur captures Delhi and founds the Mughal dynasty in India.

1530 Babur dies and his son, Humayun, succeeds him as the second Mughal ruler.

1555 Humayun reestablishes Mughal rule in India.

1556 Humayun dies unexpectedly, and his son, Akbar, age thirteen, becomes king.

1562 Akbar builds Humayun's tomb.

1565 Akbar begins building his famous Red Fort and moves the Mughal seat of power to Agra.

1569 Akbar's son Salim (Jahangir) is born.

1592 Jahangir's fifth son is born and is named Khurram (Shah Jahan) by his doting grandfather, Akbar.

1593 Arjumand Banu Baygam (Mumtaz Mahal) is born.

1605 Akbar dies and Prince Salim ascends the throne as Jahangir. He begins building Akbar's tomb.

1607 Prince Khurram is betrothed to Arjumand Banu Baygam (Mumtaz Mahal). She is Nur Jahan's niece and is the daughter of Shah Jahan's future prime minister.

1611 Jahangir marries Mihr-un-Nisa (Nur Jahan), the sister of his prime minister, and a powerful woman who rules the empire behind the scenes.

1612 Shah Jahan marries Arjumand Banu Baygam (Mumtaz Mahal).

1617 Jahangir awards Prince Khurram the name Shah Jahan, "King of the World."

1618 Aurangzeb, fifth son of Shah Jahan and Mumtaz Mahal, is born.

1627 Jahangir dies and Shah Jahan ascends the throne as the fifth Mughal emperor.

1631 While accompanying her husband on a military campaign at Burhanpur, Mumtaz Mahal dies giving birth to their fourteenth child. Shah Jahan orders the entire court into mourning for two years.

1632 Shah Jahan begins construction of Mumtaz Mahal's tomb, the Taj Mahal, which takes eleven years to complete.

1638 Shah Jahan begins work on his new capital in Delhi, called Shahjahanabad (known as Old Delhi in modern times).

1648 Shah Jahan moves the Mughal court to Delhi.

1657 Shah Jahan becomes seriously ill, and his sons begin a power struggle for the throne.

1658 Aurangzeb wins the war for succession to the throne and imprisons Shah Jahan in the Red Fort at Agra.

1666 Shah Jahan dies and is buried next to Mumtaz Mahal.

1707 Aurangzeb dies and is buried in a small tomb near the side of a road.

1700s The British expand their interests in the ports and trading posts on India's coasts.

1858 The last Mughal emperor, Bahadur Shah II, is exiled. The Mughal Empire is formally ended, and the British Raj takes over.

1898 British viceroy Lord Curzon leads the efforts to restore the Taj Mahal.

1947 India gains independence, and the new government creates two sovereign states—India and Pakistan—from the former colony based on religious beliefs.

1958 The Archaeological Survey of India is created to preserve the nation's monuments.

1993 Mahtab Garden excavation begins.

2001 The Archaeological Survey of India forms a partnership with the Taj Group of Hotels to upgrade tourist facilities and to restore the gardens of the Taj Mahal and the Mahtab Garden.

Source Notes

9   "Taj Mahal: Memorial to Love," *PBS Treasures of the World*, n.d. <http://www.pbs.org/treasuresoftheworld/a_nav/taj_nav/main_tajfrm.html> (February 7, 2003).

11 Ibid.

11 W. E. Begley and Z. A. Desai, comps. and trans., *Taj Mahal: The Illumined Tomb* (Cambridge, MA: The Aga Khan Program for Islamic Architecture, Harvard University Art Museums, 1989; distributed by University of Washington Press, Seattle), 33.

14 David Carroll and the Editors of the *Newsweek* Book Division, *The Taj Mahal* (New York: Newsweek, 1972), 31.

17 Ibid., 68.

21 Begley and Desai, *Taj Mahal: The Illumined Tomb,* 43.

23 Carroll, *The Taj Mahal*, 56–57.

23 Ibid., 58.

34 Begley and Desai, *Taj Mahal: The Illumined Tomb,* 65–66.

37 Ibid., 66.

42 Ibid., 163.

42 Ibid., 173.

42–43 Ibid., 173.

46 Ibid., 26.

58 Elizabeth B. Moynihan, ed., *The Moonlight Garden: New Discoveries at the Taj Mahal.* (Washington, D.C.: Arthur M. Sackler Gallery, Smithsonian Institution in association with University of Washington Press, Seattle, 2000), 32.

59 Ibid., 19.

61 Ibid., 28.

61 Carroll, *The Taj Mahal*, 139.

64 Moynihan, *The Moonlight Garden,* 40.

65 Ibid., 29.

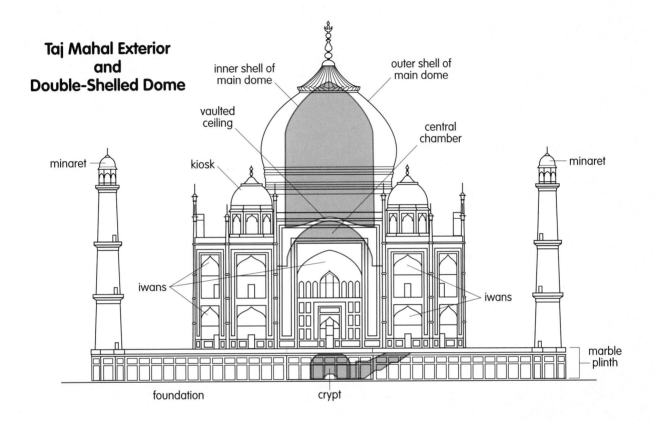

Taj Mahal Exterior and Double-Shelled Dome

inner shell of main dome

outer shell of main dome

vaulted ceiling

central chamber

minaret

kiosk

minaret

iwans

iwans

marble plinth

foundation

crypt

67 Begley and Desai, *Taj Mahal: The Illumined Tomb,* 77.

68 Moynihan, *The Moonlight Garden,* 31.

68 Ibid., 28.

76 Ibid., 134.

79 Carroll, *The Taj Mahal,* 149.

79 Rabindranath Tagore, "Shah-Jahan," *Travel to India: Taj Mahal in Agra,* n.d., <http://www.agnescv.free-online.co.uk/india/html/agra.html> (January 21 2003).

Selected Bibliography

Begley, W. E., and Z. A. Desai, comps. and trans. *Taj Mahal: The Illumined Tomb.* Cambridge, MA: The Aga Khan Program for Islamic Architecture, Harvard University Art Museums, 1989; distributed by University of Washington Press, Seattle.

Blair, Sheila S., and Jonathan M. Bloom. *The Art and Architecture of Islam, 1250–1800.* New Haven: Yale University Press, 1994.

Bloom, Jonathan M., and Sheila S. Blair. *Islamic Arts.* London: Phaidon Press Limited, 1997.

Carroll, David, and the Editors of *Newsweek* Book Division. *The Taj Mahal.* New York: Newsweek, 1972.

Fleming, John, Hugh Honour, and Nikolaus Pevsner. *The Penguin Dictionary of Architetcure.* New York: Penguin Books, 1980.

Koch, Ebba. *Mughal Architecture.* Munich, Germany: Prestel-Verlag, 1991.

Kuhnel, Ernst. *Islamic Art and Architecture.* Translated by Katherine Watson. New York: Cornell University Press, 1966.

Mark, Robert. "Architecture and Evolution," *American Scientist: The Magazine of Sigma Xi, the Scientific Research Society.* July/August 1996. Reprinted on the web at <http://www.sigmaxi.org/amsci/articles/96articles/Mark-full.html>

Moynihan, Elizabeth B., ed. *The Moonlight Garden: New Discoveries at the Taj Mahal.* Washington, D.C.: Arthur M. Sackler Gallery, Smithsonian Institution in association with University of Washington Press, Seattle, 2000.

Okada, Amina, M. C. Joshi, and Jean-Louis Nou, photographer. *Taj Mahal.* New York: Abbeville Press Publishers, 1993.

Further Reading and Websites

"Explore the Taj Mahal." *Armchair Travel Company, Ltd.***, 2000.**
<http://www.taj-mahal.net>
View short movies complete with narration and scroll across the grounds of the Taj Mahal on this virtual tour. The structure is photographed in full, both inside and out.

Hooker, Richard. "The Mughals." *Washington State University: World Civilizations*, 1996.
<http://www.wsu.edu:8080/~dee/MUGHAL/MUGHAL.HTM>
Covering everything from Mughal language to its architecture, this site is a comprehensive study of Mughal culture. It also includes a chat room for the exchange of ideas about the time.

Moorcroft, Christine. *The Taj Mahal*, Austin, TX: Steck-Vaughn, 1997.
This book is a concise history of the Taj Mahal with numerous stunning photographs of the structure.

Rothfarb, Ed. *In the Land of the Taj Mahal: The World of the Fabulous Mughals.* New York: Henry Holt & Co., 1998.
Learn all the fascinating details of Mughal life in this book, which covers a wide range of subjects including warfare, literature, and the roles of women in Mughal society.

"Taj Mahal: Memorial to Love." *PBS Treasures of the World.*
<http://www.pbs.org/treasuresoftheworld/a_nav/taj_nav/main_tajfrm.html>
This website is an interactive history of the Taj Mahal including text, photos, and sound files. Maps, paintings, and photographs are enriched by audio commentary and a brief history of Mughal art.

University of California, Los Angeles. "Culture, Architecture of India: Mughal Architecture." *Manas.*
<http://www.sscnet.ucla.edu/southasia/Culture/Archit/Mugarch.html>
This site for older readers is devoted entirely to the architecture of the Mughal dynasty. The construction of tombs, palace forts, and mosques is studied in depth.

Index

Lesley A. DuTemple has written more than a dozen books for young readers, including many award-winning titles such as her biography *Jacques Cousteau,* winner of the National Science Teachers Association/Children's Book Council Outstanding Science Trade Books for Children. After graduating from the University of California, San Diego, she attended the University of Utah's Graduate School of Architecture, where she concentrated in design and architectural history. The creator of the **Great Building Feats** series, she believes, "There's a human story behind every one of these building feats, and those stories are just as amazing as the projects themselves."

Photo Acknowledgments

The images in this book are used with the permission of: © Scala/Art Resource, NY, pp. 1, 8–9, 54–55, 73; © Royalty Free/CORBIS, pp. 2–3, 38, 48; © PhotoDisc Royalty Free, pp. 4–5; © Hulton | Archive, Getty Images, pp. 4, 8, 10, 72, 74; © Victoria & Albert Museum, London/Art Resource, NY, pp. 12, 14, 18, 22, 38–39, 40, 59, 76; © Stapleton Collection/CORBIS, p. 13; © The Art Archive/ Victoria and Albert Museum London/Sally Chappell, pp. 17, 50; © Wolfgang Kaehler, pp. 19, 43, 49, 53; © The Art Archive/Bodleian Library Oxford/The Bodleian Library, pp. 20–21 (Douce OR.b3 fol. 25), 63 (Douce a. 3 folio 24); © Diondia Picture Agency, pp. 25, 32–33, 36, 46–47 (H. Patil), 71, 78; © The Art Archive/Album/J. Enrique Molina, p. 27; © CORBIS, p. 28; © The Art Archive/British Library/British Library, p. 30; © Fine Art Photographic Library, London/Art Resource, NY, p. 35; © Mary Evans Picture Library, pp. 46, 70; © Lindsay Hebberd/CORBIS, p. 51; © The British Library, P395, p. 60; Courtesy of University of Illinois at Urbana-Champaign, College of Fine and Applied Arts, Department of Landscape Architecture, p. 62; © Historical Picture Archive/CORBIS, p. 65; © Archivo Iconographico, S. A./CORBIS, p. 66; © The Art Archive/Victoria and Albert Museum London/Eileen Tweedy, pp. 66–67; © Werner Forman/Art Resource, NY, p. 69; © Bettmann/CORBIS, p. 75. Maps and diagrams by Laura Westlund, pp. 6, 15, 24, 45 (both), 56, 67, 58, 83.

Cover photos are by: © Scala/Art Resource, NY (front) and © B. D. Rupani/ Dinodia Picture Agency (back).